Grade 4

FROM THE CLASSROOM OF
MS. WACHT

by Donna Pearson

Frank Schaffer Publications®

Author: Donna Pearson
Editor: Sara Bierling
Interior Designer: Lori Kibbey

Frank Schaffer Publications®

Send all inquiries to:
Frank Schaffer Publications
3195 Wilson Drive NW
Grand Rapids, Michigan 49534

Math 4 Today—grade 4

ISBN: 0-7682-3204-X

3 4 5 6 7 8 9 10 PAT 10 09 08 07 06

Math 4 Today

Table of Contents

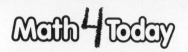

Introduction

What Is Math 4 Today?

Math 4 Today is a comprehensive yet quick and easy-to-use supplement sequenced to complement any fourth-grade math curriculum. Twenty-four essential math skills and concepts are reviewed in only ten minutes each day during a four-day period (presumably Monday through Thursday) with a 20-minute evaluation each fifth day (Friday).

How Does It Work?

Unlike many math programs, *Math 4 Today* is designed on a continuous spiral so that concepts are repeated weekly. This book supplies four problems a day for four days, covering a 40-week period based on the curricula for fourth grade. A separate ten-problem test is provided for the fifth day of each week.

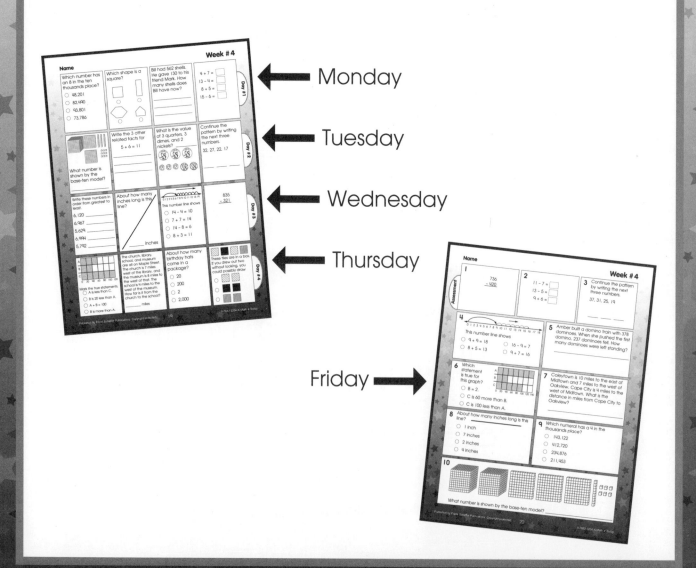

Monday

Tuesday

Wednesday

Thursday

Friday

Introduction (cont.)

Answer keys are provided for both daily drills and assessments (see pages 93–112.) Although the concepts and skills are individually categorized, most are interrelated so that many opportunities for practice and evaluation exist. A skills and concepts chart (including objectives) and a scope and sequence chart are provided.

How Was It Developed?

Math 4 Today was created in response to a need for ongoing practice after a skill had been addressed in the basal text. With the usual methods, a skill would be covered, and then almost abandoned until it reappeared (sometimes) in a six-week cumulative review. With the growing emphasis on standardized testing, the necessity for experience with test styles and semantics also becomes apparent. We began with four daily problems written on the board for students to complete while attendance was being taken. After completion, the class would briefly check and discuss the work. The problems and methods we used evolved and expanded over the years. Now, I duplicate the weekly pages for students and use overhead transparencies to check and discuss.

What Are the Benefits?

The daily approach of *Math 4 Today* provides risk-taking challenges, higher-level thinking exercises, problem-solving strategies, and necessary drills, emphasizing areas that frequently give students difficulty, such as subtraction with regrouping and word problems. The pages target test-taking skills by incorporating the style and syntax of standardized tests such as the TAKS (Texas Assessment of Knowledge and Skills). Because of its consistent format, *Math 4 Today* not only offers opportunities for instruction but also serves as an excellent diagnostic tool.

Assessment

In addition to formal assessments, ongoing informal assessment should be part of everyday instruction. This includes listening to students' responses to questions and observing students at work.

At the beginning of the school year, do a baseline assessment of each student. To do this, watch students in a variety of situations, such as at lunch, on the playground, in line, in group activities, and during individual work. An early assessment should include factors such as social (communication and cooperation), behavioral (confidence and self-control), and academic (organization and work habits) skills.

Throughout the year, you can use a variety of assessment strategies.
- questioning
- observation
- textbook tests
- teacher-developed tests
- rubrics
- student self-evaluation
- journal review
- portfolio review
- checklists
- conferences

Also, use the following assessment rubric when examining students' work. Have students become familiar with this rubric so they can do self-assessment.

3 The student's performance or work sample shows a thorough understanding of the topic. Work is clearly explained with examples and/or words, all calculations are correct, and explanations reflect reasoning beyond the simplicity of the calculations.

2 The student's performance or work sample shows a good understanding of the topic. There may be some errors in calculations, but the work reflects a general knowledge of details and a reasonable understanding of mathematical ideas.

1 The student's performance or work sample shows a limited understanding of the topic. The written work does not reflect understanding of mathematical ideas, and examples contain errors.

0 The student's performance or work sample is too weak to evaluate, or nonexistent.

Test-Taking Tips

1. Read through the entire problem before starting to solve it.

2. Use scrap paper if you need extra room to work.

3. Draw a picture, make a chart, or use symbols to help you solve.

4. Pay attention only to the important numbers in a problem.

5. Make sure you have performed the correct operation
   (+, −, x, or ÷).

6. Make sure you follow the order of operations.

7. Always show your work.

8. Read each answer choice before choosing.
   Then choose the best answer.

9. If you don't know a word, look it up or ask for help.

10. Always check your answer. Does it make sense?
    Does it answer the question?

Fill in a bubble like this: ●

not like this: ✗ ✓ ⊕

Skills and Concepts

Place Value

- identify place value to billions and thousandths
- interpret place value charts
- identify place name and value of digits
- write numeral described by place name
- read/write numerals in expanded form
- name value of specified digit in a numeral

Geometry

- distinguish between two- and three-dimensional figures
- name 2- and 3-D figures
- match congruent and similar shapes and angles
- identify lines of symmetry
- determine inclusion in overlapping shapes
- match geometric prefixes with number of sides
- find perimeter and area

Word Problems

- solve word problems using addition, subtraction, multiplication, and division
- determine operations in multi-step problems
- exclude unnecessary information
- match solution sentences to given problem
- solve word problems using whole numbers, fractions, and decimals

Computation

- practice with basic addition, subtraction, multiplication, and division facts in a singular and mixed format
- perform 2+ digit addition, subtraction, and multiplication computations with/without regrouping

Place Value Models/Fractions

- identify place value models to thousands
- name the number shown by a model representation
- draw place value models to represent a given number
- add and subtract using models with/without regrouping

Number Concepts

- write/match a solution sentence to pictured operation
- recognize fact families
- use the associative, commutative, and identity properties
- correlate addition and multiplication
- equalize multi-operational equations

Time/Money

- solve word problems with time and money
- identify coin values
- compute (+, −, x, ÷) with money
- find the amount of change due or tax involved
- express money values using $ and ¢
- create minimal collections of coins for given amounts
- interpret charts with money

Patterns/Probability

- continue a given pattern of shapes or numbers
- identify the missing element(s) in a pattern sequence
- supply a specified pattern element when the sequence immediately preceding is absent

Compare and Order Numbers

- identify or write numerical sets including decimals and fractions in order from least to greatest and vice versa with number values to billions and thousandths
- identify specific numbers in number order
- order chart information from least to greatest and vice versa

Measurement

- identify and use standard and metric units in measuring length, mass, volume, and temperature
- identify uses of measurement tools
- compare metric and standard units
- measure pictured objects within a ruled space
- measure with a nonstandard unit

Number Lines/Words

- locate numbers or a specific group of numbers on a number line
- identify missing numbers
- identify or create a number line to match a given picture or computation
- write or identify numbers or number words for given values or places to billions

Computation

- for added practice with computational skills as in row one

Graphs/Tables

- interpret, combine, and compare chart data
- construct graphs given the chart data
- interpret and construct tally charts, picture graphs, bar graphs, point and line graphs, and pie graphs
- combine and compare data

Problem Solving

- use problem-solving strategies such as logical thinking, working backward, guess and check, and drawing a picture
- solve problems with multi-step and multi-informational components
- calculate missing variables by using given information

Estimation/Reasonableness

- round numbers to tens, hundreds, and thousands
- use front-end estimation or rounding to calculate sums, differences, products, and quotients
- choose a reasonable numerical value to match a given situation (time/money situations are also included here)

Repeated Practice

- for added practice with any skill/concept included on this page or in previous lessons
- Note: Provisions for calculator use in exploring patterns, number concepts, problem solving, and estimation are indicated on the scope and sequence chart.
- for inclusion of reasonableness, estimation, or probability

Skills and Concepts

Place Value (cont.)

- compare/order digits in numbers according to place value
- determine place value to which a number has been rounded

Geometry (cont.)

- label parallel, perpendicular, or intersecting lines
- count angles, vertices, faces, and edges of plane & solid figures
- identify hexagon, pentagon, polygon, prism, rhombus, parallelogram, trapezoid, quadrilateral, as well as equilateral, isosceles, and scalene triangles
- distinguish among flips, slides, and turns

Word Problems (cont.)

- identify information needed to solve a problem
- match solution sentences to given problem
- match common clue words to operations
- use concepts of time and money to solve problems
- use calculator to assist and verify solutions

Computation (cont.)

- divide 2+ digit numerals with/without remainders and with 1+ digit divisors
- compute using zeros in all operations
- add 2+ digit columns with/without regrouping
- check subtraction with addition and vice versa
- supply missing addends, multipliers, and divisors

Place Value Models/Fractions (cont.)

- use decimal representations for addition, subtraction, and multiplication
- identify fractional parts of shaded figures and/or sets
- compare/equalize/simplify fractions with/without picture representation
- add, subtract, and multiply fractions and mixed numbers

Number Concepts (cont.)

- supply missing addends
- use non-equality in equations
- identify true and non-true equations
- calculate mean, median, range, and mode
- apply greatest common factor and least common multiple
- perform operations with exponents

Time/Money (cont.)

- determine comparative money values
- compute portion when given a set group value
- identify clock face time by hour, half-hour, and minute intervals
- determine elapsed time using clocks
- determine elapsed time in word problems

Patterns/Probability (cont.)

- describe the rule for a pattern sequence
- create a pattern using specified units
- visualize pattern to designated conclusion
- continue situational patterns
- investigate patterns with calculator

Compare and Order Numbers (cont.)

- use the inequality symbols > and < to compare numbers
- choose a group of numbers according to a specified order
- use odd and even numbers, skip counting, and number patterns in ordering
- compare and order units of standard and metric measurements

Measurement (cont.)

- compare given measurements
- use a ruler to measure the perimeter of given shapes
- estimate situational uses with the appropriate unit
- determine area, volume, and perimeter with/without all dimensions given
- find equivalent measurements
- use symmetry and congruence in calculating measurements
- enlarge to scale using grids

Number Lines/Words (cont.)

- match equations to number line representation
- locate representative points for fractions/decimals on a number line
- write or match words for fractions and decimals

Computation (cont.)

Graphs/Tables (cont.)

- use symbols having a value of more than 1 unit and of half a unit
- write questions regarding a graph
- determine unit of comparison in a graph
- write concise summary of graph data
- plot number pairs
- give number pair location of a symbol on a grid

Problem Solving (cont.)

- choose possible solutions given indefinite variables
- select an amount large enough to include the combined variables given
- order objects or numbers in sequence given non-sequential variables
- write questions for given solutions regarding data available

Estimation/ Reasonableness (cont.)

- round decimals to nearest hundredth, tenth, or whole number
- select equations for best estimate of given values
- visually estimate comparative sizes
- use calculations to verify estimates

Repeated Practice (cont.)

Skills and Concepts

Place Value (cont.)

Geometry (cont.)

- select figures with specified characteristics
- classify right, acute, obtuse, and corresponding angles
- name by identifying points: line, segment, ray, chord, radius, diameter, and circumference

Word Problems (cont.)

- apply problem-solving strategies and concept development

Computation (cont.)

- add, subtract, and multiply fractions/mixed fractions
- add, subtract, multiply, and divide decimals to thousandths
- use calculator to verify computations

Place Value Models/Fractions (cont.)

- utilize common denominators in computations
- find ratios/equivalent ratios
- identify decimal values to thousandths
- compare decimals to fractional parts
- find equivalent decimals
- add, subtract, multiply, and divide decimals

Number Concepts (cont.)

- use order of operations in multi-computational equations
- label prime and composite numbers
- complete factor trees

Time/Money (cont.)

- recognize values of standard time units
- determine equivalent measures of time
- interpret schedules
- designate AM or PM

Patterns/Probability (cont.)

- choose possible outcomes or non-inclusion in a given set of conditions
- write probability in fractional terms
- compare probability in different sets and in multi-chance situations
- compute simple odds

Compare and Order Numbers (cont.)

Measurement (cont.)

- measure length, area, and perimeter using 1/2 units
- identify formulas for finding area and perimeter
- find area and circumference of circles

Number Lines/Words (cont.)

Computation (cont.)

Graphs/Tables (cont.)

- determine number pair inclusion in overlapping shapes on a grid
- interpret calendars
- plot number pairs
- give number pair location of a symbol on a grid

Problem Solving (cont.)

- solve for *n* in equations
- complete logic problems using process of elimination
- classify according to given descriptors
- write questions for given solutions regarding data available

Estimation/ Reasonableness (cont.)

Repeated Practice (cont.)

0-7682-3204-X *Math 4 Today*

Scope and Sequence

Skill and Concepts	1	T	2	T	3	T	4	T	5	T	6	T	7	T	8	T	9	T	10	T	11	T	12	T	13	T	14	T	15	T	16	T	17	T	18	T	19	T	20	T
1 Place Value	•	•	•	•	•	•	•	•	•	•	•	•	•	•	•	•	•	•	•	•	•	•	•	•	•	•	•	•	•	•	•	•	•	•	•	•	•	•	•	•
2 Geometry	•	•	•	•	•	•	•		•	•	•	•											•		•		•		•		•	•	•	•	•	•	•	•	•	
3 Word Problems	•	•	•	•	•	•	•	•	•	•	•		•	•	•	•	•	•	•	•	•		•	•	•	•	•	•	•	•	•	•	•	•	•	•	•	•	•	•
4 Basic Facts	•	•	•	•	•	•	•	•	•	•	•		•		•		•	•	•	•			•		•		•		•	•	•	•	•	•	•	•		•		•
5 Addition	•	•	•		•	•	•	•	•	•	•																•	•										•		
6 Subtraction	•	•	•	•	•	•	•		•	•	•	•	•	•							•		•			•	•	•	•	•	•	•	•	•	•	•	•	•	•	•
7 Multiplication					•	•	•	•	•		•																						•	•	•		•	•	•	•
8 Division																																	•							
9 Place Value Models	•		•		•		•		•		•		•		•		•				•		•		•		•		•		•		•		•		•			
10 Fractions																																								
11 Decimals																																	•							
12 Number Concepts	•	•	•	•	•	•	•	•	•	•	•	•	•	•	•	•	•	•	•	•	•	•	•	•	•	•	•	•	•	•	•	•	•	•	•	•	•	•	•	•
13 Time					•	•	•	•					•	•	•	•	•	•			•				•		•		•	•	•		•		•		•	•	•	•
14 Money	•		•		•	•	•		•	•	•		•	•	•	•	•	•	•	•	•		•		•		•	•	•		•	•	•	•	•		•	•	•	•
15 Patterns	•	•	•		•		•	•	•		•	•	•	•	•	•	•		•		•	•	•		•	•	•	•	•	•	•	•	•	•	•	•	•	•	•	•
16 Compare/Order Numbers			•		•	•	•	•	•	•	•	•	•		•		•	•	•	•	•	•	•		•		•	•	•	•	•	•	•	•	•	•	•	•	•	
17 Measurement	•		•		•	•	•	•	•		•	•	•						•				•		•		•		•		•		•		•		•	•	•	•
18 Number Lines			•		•		•												•		•		•		•		•		•		•		•		•		•			
19 Number Words	•	•	•	•	•	•	•		•	•	•	•	•	•	•	•	•	•	•	•	•	•	•	•	•	•	•	•	•	•	•	•	•	•	•		•	•	•	•
20 Graphs/Tables	•	•	•	•	•	•	•		•		•	•	•	•	•		•	•	•	•	•		•	•	•	•	•	•	•	•	•	•	•	•	•	•	•	•	•	•
21 Problem Solving	•	•	•	•	•	•	•	•	•	•	•	•	•	•	•	•	•	•	•	•	•	•	•		•		•	•	•	•	•	•	•	•	•	•	•	•	•	•
22 Estimation	•		•		•		•		•				•		•		•		•												•		•		•		•		•	•
23 Reasonableness	•		•	•	•	•	•	•	•	•									•		•		•		•		•													
24 Probability							•		•		•																•		•										•	
25 Repeated Practice/Calculator Opportunity															•						•												•		•					

T = Weekly Test   • Indicates Skill or Concept Included and/or Tested

0-7682-3204-X *Math 4 Today*

Scope and Sequence

Skill and Concepts	21	T	22	T	23	T	24	T	25	T	26	T	27	T	28	T	29	T	30	T	31	T	32	T	33	T	34	T	35	T	36	T	37	T	38	T	39	T	40	T
1 Place Value	•	•	•	•	•	•	•	•	•	•	•	•	•	•	•	•	•	•	•	•	•	•	•	•	•	•	•	•	•	•	•	•	•	•	•	•	•	•	•	•
2 Geometry	•	•	•	•	•	•	•	•	•	•	•		•			•	•	•	•	•	•	•	•	•	•	•	•	•	•	•	•	•	•	•	•	•	•	•	•	•
3 Word Problems	•	•	•	•	•	•		•	•	•	•	•	•	•	•	•	•	•	•	•	•	•	•	•	•	•	•	•	•	•	•	•	•	•	•	•	•	•	•	•
4 Basic Facts																									•		•		•		•		•		•		•		•	
5 Addition		•					•	•	•	•	•	•	•	•	•	•	•	•	•	•	•	•	•	•	•	•	•	•	•	•	•	•	•	•	•	•	•	•	•	•
6 Subtraction		•		•			•	•			•		•		•	•	•	•	•	•	•	•	•	•	•	•	•	•	•	•	•	•	•		•	•	•	•	•	•
7 Multiplication	•		•	•	•	•	•		•	•	•	•	•	•	•	•	•		•	•	•	•	•	•	•	•	•	•	•	•	•	•	•	•	•	•	•		•	•
8 Division				•			•				•		•	•	•	•	•			•	•		•	•			•	•	•	•	•	•	•	•	•	•	•	•	•	•
9 Place Value Models	•									•																														
10 Fractions		•	•	•		•	•	•	•	•	•	•	•	•	•	•	•	•	•	•	•		•	•	•	•	•	•	•	•	•	•	•	•	•	•	•	•	•	•
11 Decimals																						•		•								•							•		
12 Number Concepts	•		•	•				•	•				•		•	•	•		•	•	•		•		•		•		•		•		•		•		•		•	
13 Time	•				•	•	•			•	•		•	•	•	•	•			•	•	•	•	•	•		•	•			•			•					•	
14 Money	•		•		•	•		•						•	•	•	•	•	•			•	•	•	•		•	•	•		•		•		•	•	•			•
15 Patterns	•			•	•	•			•	•		•	•	•	•	•	•	•		•				•																
16 Compare/Order Numbers	•	•	•	•	•	•	•	•	•			•	•	•	•	•	•	•	•	•	•		•		•	•	•			•	•		•		•					•
17 Measurement		•	•	•	•	•	•		•		•		•	•	•	•	•		•		•		•		•	•	•				•		•			•	•			•
18 Number Lines		•	•	•	•									•			•	•			•	•	•	•								•		•				•		
19 Number Words	•					•				•			•		•	•	•	•			•		•		•	•	•		•	•	•	•	•	•	•		•		•	•
20 Graphs/Tables	•		•	•	•	•			•	•	•	•	•	•	•	•	•	•	•	•	•		•	•	•	•	•	•	•	•	•	•	•	•	•	•	•	•	•	•
21 Problem Solving	•		•	•	•	•			•	•	•	•	•	•	•	•	•	•	•	•	•	•	•	•	•	•	•	•	•		•	•	•		•		•	•	•	•
22 Estimation	•		•	•	•	•	•		•		•		•	•	•	•	•	•	•		•	•	•	•	•		•	•	•	•	•		•		•		•	•	•	•
23 Reasonableness					•						•		•				•		•		•						•		•		•	•	•		•	•	•		•	
24 Probability	•		•	•	•	•	•					•		•		•						•			•									•						
25 Repeated Practice/ Calculator Opportunity															•		•												•					•				•		•

0-7682-3204-X *Math 4 Today*

Which number has a 3 in the hundreds place?

○ 231

○ 390

○ 803

○ 730

Which shape is a triangle?

One of the largest jigsaw puzzles was built in Oklahoma and measured 48 feet long. Compared to an average jigsaw puzzle, which measures about 2 feet long, how much longer was the Oklahoma puzzle?

_____

4 + 7 = ☐

2 + 9 = ☐

8 + 5 = ☐

7 + 7 = ☐

Day #1

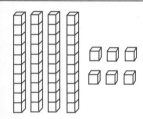

What number is shown by the base-ten model?

_____

Write the family of facts for 8, 6, and 14.

_____

_____

_____

_____

Show how to find the value of five dimes and four pennies.

_____

_____

_____

Continue the pattern by writing the next three numbers.

8, 10, 12, 14

____ ____ ____

Day #2

Write these numbers in order from least to greatest.

89   _____

72   _____

105 _____

68   _____

94   _____

About how many inches tall is the music note?

_____ inches

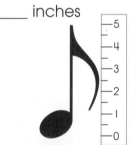

This number line shows

○ 8 – 7 = 1

○ 5 + 8 = 13

○ 2 + 3 = 5

○ 5 – 5 = 0

12 – 7 = ☐

11 – 9 = ☐

13 – 5 = ☐

16 – 8 = ☐

Day #3

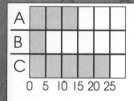

0 5 10 15 20 25

This graph shows

A = _____ B = _____

C = _____

In a roll of candy, the grape is before the cherry. There are two candies between cherry and lime. The orange is next to the lime, and the lemon is last. Color the candies in the correct order.

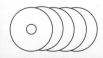

About how many television programs are on one channel between 6:00 and 10:00 at night?

○ 8

○ 80

○ 800

○ 8,000

Side 1   Side 2

The drawing above shows both sides of one chip. If you tossed the above chip one time, which would NOT be a possible way for it to land?

○ ○ ○

Day #4

Assessment

1

$8 + 5 = \boxed{}$

$9 + 2 = \boxed{}$

$6 + 7 = \boxed{}$

2

$15 - 8 = \boxed{}$

$14 - 5 = \boxed{}$

$17 - 9 = \boxed{}$

3 About how many pieces of mail might one family receive in a day?

○ 6,000

○ 600

○ 60

○ 6

4 One of the largest beds was built in 1430 in Belgium. The bed was 19 feet long. Today, an average bed is about 6 feet long. How much longer was the bed built in 1430?

_____

5 Write the family of facts for 3, 6, and 9.

_____

_____

_____

_____

6 Write these numbers in order from least to greatest.

50 _____

65 _____

89 _____

85 _____

79 _____

7 Which number has a 2 in the tens place?

○ 921

○ 192

○ 2

○ 209

8 Which shape is a triangle?

○

○

○

○

9 Show how to find the value of six dimes and eight pennies.

_____

_____

_____

10 What numbers are shown by the base-ten models?

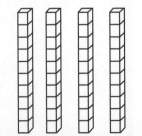
_____

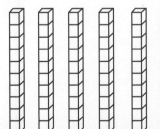
_____

Day #1

In the number 673

the _____ is in the tens place.

the _____ is in the hundreds place.

the _____ is in the ones place.

Which shape is a cube?

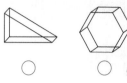

○　○

○　○

Rashana had 16 children's picture books. She gave 9 of them to her younger cousin. How many picture books does Rashana have now? (Show your solution number sentence.)

_____

_____

$6 + 6 =$ ☐

$7 + 7 =$ ☐

$8 + 8 =$ ☐

$9 + 9 =$ ☐

Day #2

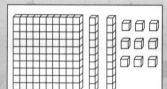

What number is shown by the base-ten model?

_____

Write the fact family for 6, 4, and 10.

_____

_____

_____

What is the value of

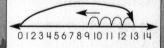

4 dimes and 2 nickels?

_____ ¢

Continue the pattern by writing the next three numbers.

55, 60, 65, 70

_____ _____ _____

Day #3

Write these numbers in order from greatest to least.

120 _____

920 _____

617 _____

912 _____

198 _____

About how many inches long is this arrow?

_____ inches

---

0 1 2 3 4 5 6 7 8 9 10 11 12 13 14

This number line shows:

○ $14 - 4 = 10$

○ $13 + 1 = 14$

○ $13 - 9 = 4$

○ $13 - 4 = 9$

$14 - 9 =$ ☐

$15 - 9 =$ ☐

$16 - 9 =$ ☐

$17 - 9 =$ ☐

Day #4

Spelling Test Grades

Jana

Karen

Amy

Which two girls have spelling test grades that are about the same?

_____ _____

Mystery Number

I am a number between 10 and 20. You can add 2 to me and get the number that is the sum of 7 and 9. What number am I?

_____

About how many chocolate-coated candies come in a small package?

○ 3

○ 30

○ 300

○ 3,000

These cubes are in a box. If you drew one out without looking, you would most likely draw a

○ ▪

○ ◻

Assessment

1

5 + 5 = ☐

9 + 9 = ☐

7 + 7 = ☐

2

11 – 9 = ☐

13 – 4 = ☐

15 – 9 = ☐

3 Continue the pattern by writing the next three numbers.

35, 40, 45, 50

_____ _____ _____

4

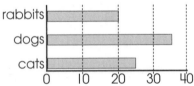

This number line shows

○ 9 + 9 = 18   ○ 8 + 5 = 13

○ 17 – 8 = 9   ○ 17 – 10 = 7

5 Nina bought 17 peppermints. She shared 8 of them with her friends. How many peppermints does Nina have now? _____

6 Fourth Grade's Favorite Pets

Which two pets received about the same number of votes? _____ _____

7 Mystery Number

I am an even number between 10 and 30. You can add 4 to me and get the sum of 10 and 10. What number am I?

_____

8 About how many inches long is the line?

about _____ inches long

9 In the number 842

the _____ is in the ones place.

the _____ is in the hundreds place.

the _____ is in the tens place.

10

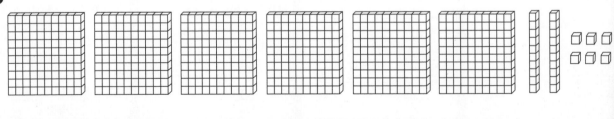

What number is shown by the base-ten model? _____

0-7682-3204-X *Math 4 Today*

Name

Day #1

Which number has a 6 in the hundreds place?

○ 46,201

○ 62,490

○ 93,601

○ 93,716

Which shape is a rectangle?

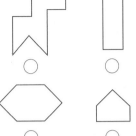

Fran has 459 stamps in her collection. Erica has 969 stamps in her collection. Show how many more stamps Erica has than Fran.

_____

$8 + 7 =$ ☐

$12 - 4 =$ ☐

$9 + 5 =$ ☐

$13 - 7 =$ ☐

Day #2

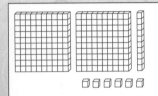

What number is shown by the base-ten model?

_____

Write the family of facts for 5, 9, and 14.

_____

_____

_____

_____

Show how to find the value of two quarters, three dimes, and four nickels.

Continue the pattern by writing the next three numbers.

4, 7, 10, 13

____ ____ ____

Day #3

Write these numbers in order from least to greatest.

620 _____

696 _____

602 _____

599 _____

679 _____

About how many inches tall is the paintbrush?

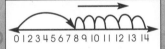

_____ inches

This number line shows

○ $14 - 7 = 7$

○ $8 + 8 = 16$

○ $14 - 8 = 6$

○ $8 + 6 = 14$

235
+ 524

Day #4

Shade in the graph to show

A = 60   B = 20

C = A + B

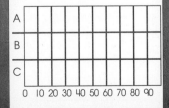

Jack, Sam, and Ed live on the same road. Sam lives 7 miles east of Jack. Ed lives 13 east of Jack. How far does Ed live from Sam?

_____ miles

About how many pages are in your spelling book?

○ 50

○ 500

○ 5

○ 150

The numerals 1, 2, 3, 4, 5, and 6 are on a die. If you rolled the die two times, which would NOT be a possible combination?

○ 2, 3

○ 5, 5

○ 6, 7

○ 1, 6

Assessment

1

$$756$$
$$+\ 253$$

2

15 – 8 = ☐

14 – 5 = ☐

6 + 7 = ☐

3 About how many pages are in a child's picture book?

○ 1,000

○ 10

○ 100

○ 1

4 Ben has 562 baseball cards. Al has 783 baseball cards. Show how to find how many more baseball cards Al has.

_____

5 Write the family of facts for 8, 9, and 17.

_____ _____

_____ _____

6 Write these numbers in order from least to greatest.

850 _____

865 _____

895 _____

856 _____

799 _____

7 Which number has a 9 in the tens place?

○ 907

○ 192

○ 9,517

○ 829

8 Which shape is a rectangle?

○

○

○

○

9 Show how to find the value of 7 dimes, 3 quarters, and 6 nickels.

10

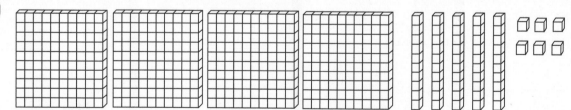

What number is shown by the base-ten model? _____

0-7682-3204-X *Math 4 Today*

Day #1

Which number has an 8 in the ten thousands place?

○ 48,201

○ 82,490

○ 93,801

○ 73,786

Which shape is a square?

Bill had 562 shells. He gave 130 to his friend Mark. How many shells does Bill have now?

_____

_____

_____

---

4 + 7 = ☐

13 – 4 = ☐

8 + 5 = ☐

15 – 6 = ☐

Day #2

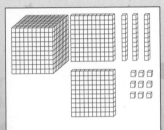

What number is shown by the base-ten model?

_____

Write the 3 other related facts for

5 + 6 = 11

_____

_____

_____

What is the value of 3 quarters, 3 dimes, and 2 nickels? _____

Continue the pattern by writing the next three numbers.

32, 27, 22, 17

____ ____ ____

Day #3

Write these numbers in order from greatest to least.

6,120 _____

6,967 _____

5,629 _____

6,994 _____

5,792 _____

About how many inches long is this line?

_____ inches

---

0 1 2 3 4 5 6 7 8 9 10 11 12 13 14

This number line shows

○ 14 – 4 = 10

○ 7 + 7 = 14

○ 14 – 8 = 6

○ 8 + 3 = 11

835
– 321

Day #4

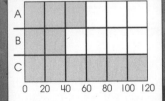

Mark the true statements.
○ A is less than C.
○ B is 20 less than A.
○ A + B = 100
○ B is more than A.

The church, library, school, and museum are all on Maple Street. The church is 7 miles west of the library, and the museum is 8 miles to the west of that. The school is 4 miles to the west of the museum. How far is it from the church to the school?

_____ miles

About how many birthday hats come in a package?

○ 20

○ 200

○ 2

○ 2,000

These tiles are in a box. If you drew out two without looking, you could possibly draw

○

○

○

Assessment

1

$$736$$
$$- 420$$

2

$11 - 7 = \boxed{}$

$13 - 5 = \boxed{}$

$9 + 6 = \boxed{}$

3 Continue the pattern by writing the next three numbers.

37, 31, 25, 19

____ ____ ____

4

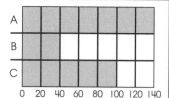

This number line shows

○ $9 + 9 = 18$ ○ $16 - 9 = 7$

○ $8 + 5 = 13$ ○ $9 + 7 = 16$

5 Amber built a domino train with 378 dominoes. When she pushed the first domino, 237 dominoes fell. How many dominoes were left standing?

_____

6 Which statement is true for this graph?

A
B
C
0 20 40 60 80 100 120 140

○ B = 2.

○ C is 60 more than B.

○ C is 100 less than A.

7 Coleytown is 10 miles to the east of Midtown and 7 miles to the west of Oakview. Cape City is 4 miles to the west of Midtown. What is the distance in miles from Cape City to Oakview?

_____

8 About how many inches long is this line? _____

○ 1 inch

○ 7 inches

○ 2 inches

○ 4 inches

9 Which numeral has a 4 in the thousands place?

○ 143,122

○ 412,720

○ 234,876

○ 211,453

10

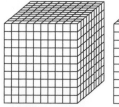 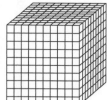 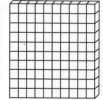 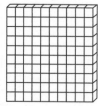 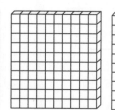

What number is shown by the base-ten model? _____

Day #1

Which number has a 4 in the ten thousands place and a 6 in the hundreds place?

○ 418,601

○ 342,690

○ 249,861

○ 763,486

Match.

pentagon _____

octagon _____

hexagon _____

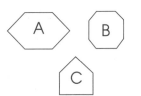

Jen has a total of 762 reading points. Last year, she had 512 points. How many more points has she earned so far this year?

_____

5 x 7 = ☐

17 – 8 = ☐

3 x 4 = ☐

11 – 6 = ☐

Day #2

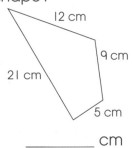

After adding 6 more units to this model, the number shown would be _____.

Which fact does not belong in this set?

○ 7 + 6 = 13

○ 6 + 6 = 12

○ 13 – 7 = 6

○ 13 – 6 = 7

Kyle bought a game for $8.53. He had $9.85 in his wallet before he paid for the game. How much money does he have now?

_____

Continue the pattern by writing the next two numbers.

113, 223, 333, 443

_____ _____

Day #3

Use > or < to compare.

63,120 ☐ 63,225

5,967 ☐ 5,987

35,629 ☐ 4,629

8,094 ☐ 80,003

What is the perimeter of this shape?

12 cm

9 cm

21 cm

5 cm

_____ cm

Write the numbers for the number words.

sixty-one thousand, four hundred twenty-five

_____

three hundred seventy thousand, nine hundred forty-two

_____

345
+ 228

Day #4

Students with Perfect Attendance

Grade	1996	1997
3	95	103
4	87	92
5	92	93
6	82	105

For which grade was perfect attendance about the same in both years? _____

Mystery Numbers

A = B x 2
B = C + C
C = 13 – 8
D = A – C

A = _____

B = _____

C = _____

D = _____

Solve using front-end estimation.

2,734
3,120
1,256
+ 3,607

If you pitched a penny 50 times onto the board below, the penny would most likely land on the numeral _____ most often.

1	3	5	7
9	5	2	4
6	8	0	5

Assessment

1
```
  736
+ 225
```

2
$5 \times 6 =$ ☐

$17 - 9 =$ ☐

$4 \times 4 =$ ☐

3 Solve using front-end estimation.
```
  4,298
  3,170
  1,569
+ 2,890
```

4 Pete bowled a total score of 578 in four games. His score for the first three games was 436. What was his score for the last game he bowled?

_____

5 Which pair are NOT related facts?

○ $6 + 7 = 13$ $7 + 6 = 13$

○ $12 - 7 = 5$ $5 + 7 = 12$

○ $11 - 8 = 3$ $11 - 3 = 8$

○ $14 - 6 = 8$ $7 + 7 = 14$

6 Use > or < to compare.

54,239 ☐ 5,982

8,230 ☐ 8,159

29,451 ☐ 29,743

7,291 ☐ 7,192

7 Which number has a 7 in the thousands place and a 2 in the tens place?

○ 372,719

○ 187,320

○ 822,702

○ 728,206

8 Match.

square _____

cube _____

cylinder _____

rectangle _____

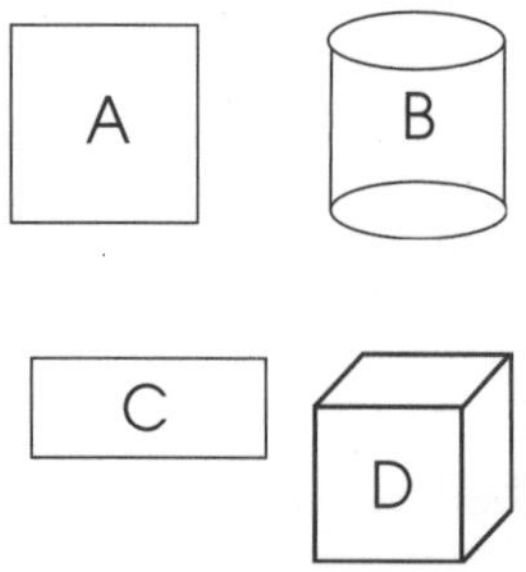

A   B

C   D

9 Jack saved $9.67 for a model kit. The kit was on sale for $8.50. How much money will Jack have leftover after buying the model kit?

_____

10

City	New Students Enrolled	
	1997	1998
Decatur	327	452
Lennox	678	701
Bingum	239	251
Coxton	455	592

Which city's new student enrollment stayed closest to the same between the years 1997 and 1998? _____

Day #1

In the number 872,391,

the 7 is in the _____ place.

the 3 is in the _____ place.

the 8 is in the _____ place.

Circle the shape that best represents a rectangular prism.

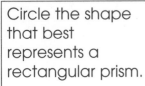
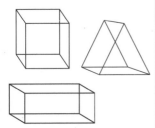

The student council sold 32 cupcakes and 25 brownies at the bake sale. They also sold 12 pies. How many baked goods did the student council sell? Show your solution number sentence.

_____

_____

---

4 x 2 = ☐

11 – 8 = ☐

3 x 3 = ☐

15 – 6 = ☐

Day #2

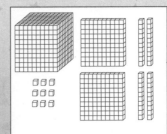

After adding 7 more tens to this model, the number shown would be _____.

Which is NOT a related fact?

○ 9 + 3 = 12

○ 3 + 9 = 12

○ 12 – 7 = 5

○ 12 – 9 = 3

Jim spent $4.13 on a model kit and 2 quarters to play a video game. Show how to find the total amount of money Jim spent.

_____

_____

Continue the pattern by writing the next three numbers.

220, 215, 210, 205

_____ _____ _____

Day #3

Use > or < to compare.

23,534 ☐ 23,530

9,967 ☐ 3,987

75,629 ☐ 104,629

894 ☐ 8,004

What is the perimeter of this shape? _____

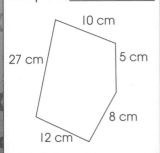

10 cm

27 cm

5 cm

8 cm

12 cm

Write the number for the number words.

two hundred five thousand, one hundred nineteen

_____

nine hundred thousand, six hundred five

_____

2,757
+ 6,229

Day #4

Grade	Number of Boys	Girls
3	115	103
4	98	92
5	125	112
6	107	111

Which grade has 10 more boys than grade 3? _____

Mystery Numbers

A = C – D

B = D – 2

C = B + B

D = the difference between 24 and 14

A = _____   B = _____

C = _____   D = _____

Solve using front-end estimation.

23,734
42,120
12,256
+ 15,607

If you pitched a penny 20 times onto the board below, the penny would most likely land on the numbers _____ and the least often on _____.

7	3	5	7
7	5	2	7
5	2	1	5

Assessment

1

4,609
+ 3,285

2

2 x 6 = ☐

11 – 3 = ☐

3 x 5 = ☐

3 Continue the pattern by writing the next three numbers.

206, 203, 200, 197

_____ _____ _____

4 Write the number for the number words.

two hundred seventy-one thousand, four hundred nine _____

one hundred four thousand, three hundred six _____

5 Which pair are NOT related facts?

○ 2 + 7 = 9   9 – 6 = 3

○ 12 – 9 = 3   3 + 9 = 12

○ 9 – 8 = 1   9 – 1 = 8

○ 10 – 6 = 4   6 + 4 = 10

6

Team Scores in Weekly Bowling Tournament

Day	Stars	Jets
Saturday	327	152
Sunday	478	599
Wednesday	432	557
Friday	455	422

On which day did the Jets have 125 more points than the Stars? _____

7 Hannah spent $1.25 on popcorn and 6 dimes on candy at the movies. Show how to find the amount of money she spent.

_____

8 What is the perimeter of this shape?

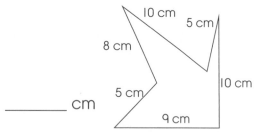

10 cm 5 cm 8 cm 10 cm 5 cm 9 cm

_____ cm

9 In the number 568,120,

the 8 is in the _____ place.

the 2 is in the _____ place.

the 5 is in the _____ place.

10

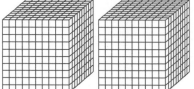 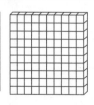 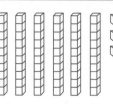

After adding 8 more tens to this model, the number shown would be _____

0-7682-3204-X *Math 4 Today*

For each number below, write the digit that is in the ten thousands place first and the digit that is in the ten millions place second.

234,459,880 _____

_____

54,182,635 _____

_____

Which letter is in the triangle and circle but not in the square? _____

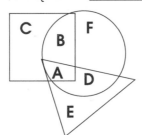

Lane did 37 math problems on Monday. He worked 48 more problems on Tuesday. How many math problems did Lane work on during these two days?

_____

$14 - \boxed{} = 7$

$11 - \boxed{} = 8$

$3 + \boxed{} = 12$

$6 + \boxed{} = 15$

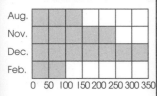

After subtracting 3 tens from this model, the number shown would be _____

Put a checkmark next to the other names for 21.

_____ 9 + 10

_____ 3 x 7

_____ 1 ten, 2 ones

_____ 2 tens, 1 one

_____ 10 + 11

_____ 6 + 6 + 6 + 3

_____ 25 – 5

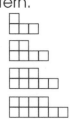

What time is shown on this clock? _____

Draw the tenth pattern.

Which group of numbers is in order from least to greatest?

○ 254, 165, 138, 97

○ 889, 976, 981, 872

○ 567, 475, 330, 290

○ 654, 678, 732, 751

About how tall is the candle?

○ 3 cm

○ $3\frac{1}{2}$ cm

○ 5 cm

○ $4\frac{1}{2}$ cm

This number line shows

○ 12 + 3 = 15

○ 12 – 3 = 9

○ 12 – 9 = 3

$$\begin{array}{r} 752 \\ + 289 \\ \hline \end{array}$$

Number of Patrons in a Toy Store

Aug.							
Nov.							
Dec.							
Feb.							

0 50 100 150 200 250 300 350

In which month did more than 300 patrons visit the store? _____

Bill is 2 inches taller than Sam. Sam is shorter than Joe. Roy is 4 inches taller than Tyler. What information do you need to find out Roy's height?

○ Sam's height

○ Joe's height

○ Tyler's height

Round each number to the nearest ten.

23 → _____

42 → _____

18 → _____

87 → _____

Which shows the most accurate way to estimate the sum of 3,452 and 5,321?

○ 5,321 – 3,452

○ 3,400 + 5,300

○ 3,000 + 5,000

Assessment

1

667
+ 285

2

$2 + \boxed{} = 3$

$7 + \boxed{} = 15$

$15 - \boxed{} = 9$

3 Round to the nearest ten.

26 → _____

83 → _____

92 → _____

4 Ben collected 89 aluminum cans on Saturday. He collected 18 more cans on Sunday. How many cans did Ben collect on Saturday and Sunday?

_____

5 What are other names for 35?

○ 3 + 5

○ 3 tens, 5 ones

○ 5 x 7

○ 50 – 3

6 Which group of numbers is in order from least to greatest?

○ 534, 567, 572

○ 743, 778, 723

○ 248, 238, 223

7 For each number below, write the digit that is in the one millions place first and the digit that is in the thousands place second.

245,329,017 _____

_____

520,291,386 _____

_____

8 Which letter is in the square and rectangle but not in the circle? _____

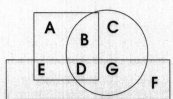

9 What time is shown on this clock? _____

10

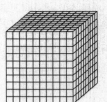

After subtracting 6 tens from this model, the number shown would be _____.

Name

Day #1

For each number below, write the digit in the ten thousands place first and the digit in the hundred millions place second.

831,459,620 _____

_____

954,182,635 _____

_____

Which letter is in the triangle, circle, and rectangle, but not in the square? _____

Marty's kite flew 254 decimeters high. Andy's kite flew 876 decimeters high. How much higher did Andy's kite fly?

_____

```
  752
  524
+ 236
```

Day #2

Use the model to show how to subtract 9 ones. What number is left? _____

Use >, <, or = to compare.

8 + 4 [ ] 2 x 6

13 – 5 [ ] 7 + 7

9 x 5 [ ] 5 x 9

4 x 4 [ ] 9 + 4

What time is shown on this clock? _____

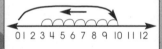

Draw the sixth pattern in the empty box.

○ ○ ○ ○ ○
○ ○ ○ ○ ○
○ ○ ○ ○ ○
● ● ● ● ●
● ● ● ● ●
● ● ● ● ●
○ ○ ○ ○ ○
○ ○ ○ ○ ○
○ ○ ○ ○ ○
○ ○ ○ ○ ○
● ● ● ● ●
● ● ● ● ●

Day #3

City Streets	Length
Bok Ave.	52,400 m
Syl St.	23,452 m
Lyd Blvd.	47,220 m
Nox St.	59,198 m

Name the streets in order of length from greatest to least.

_____

_____

_____

_____

About how long is the leaf?

○ 9 cm

○ 5 ½ cm

○ 6 cm

○ 7 ½ cm

This number line shows

○ 3 + 7 = 10

○ 10 – 3 = 7

○ 10 – 7 = 3

```
  392
– 269
```

Day #4

Child	Allowance
Tim	○○○○○○
Beth	○○○
Sal	○○○○○
Jake	○○○○

each ○ = 10¢

Who earned 20¢ more than Beth? _____.

Don ate 4 slices of pizza. Greg ate less pizza than Stan. Tom ate 2 more slices than Greg. To find out how much pizza was eaten by Tom, you need to know the number of slices eaten by

○ Stan

○ Greg

○ Don

Round each number to the nearest hundred.

253 → _____

412 → _____

183 → _____

87 → _____

Which shows the most accurate way to estimate the difference between 521 and 412?

○ 500 – 400

○ 412 + 521

○ 520 – 410

Assessment

1

```
  365
  121
+ 557
```

2

```
  962
- 124
```

3 What is the most accurate estimate of the difference between 862 and 747?

- ○ 747 + 862
- ○ 800 – 700
- ○ 860 – 750
- ○ 900 – 700

4

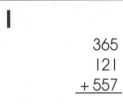

Write the number sentence shown by this number line.

_____

5 The bookshelves in Mrs. Kim's class are 671 centimeters tall. Mr. Derrick's shelves are 832 centimeters tall. How much taller are the shelves in Mr. Derrick's classroom?

_____

6 Which graph shows that Mary planted 10 more flowers than Sue? _____

Beth	❀ ❀
Jill	❀ ❀ ❀ ❀ ❀
Mary	❀ ❀ ❀ ❀ ❀
Sue	❀ ❀ ❀
❀ = 5	

Graph A

Beth	❀
Jill	❀ ❀ ❀
Mary	❀ ❀ ❀ ❀ ❀
Sue	❀ ❀ ❀
❀ = 2	

Graph B

7 Kelly earned $5.00. Annie earned $2.00 more than Liz. Gina earned less than Liz. To find out how much money Annie earned, you need to know the amount of money earned by

○ Liz   ○ Gina   ○ Kelly

8 How many centimeters long is the bead pattern?

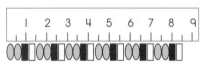

- ○ 10 cm
- ○ $8\frac{1}{2}$ cm
- ○ $9\frac{1}{2}$ cm
- ○ 6 cm

9 For each number, write the digit that is in the millions place first and the digit that is in the hundred thousands place second.

254,307,199 _____ _____

589,620,413 _____ _____

10 Round each number to the nearest hundred.

197 → _____

231 → _____

552 → _____

Day # 1

Write each number in expanded form.

259,341 _____

_____

182,635 _____

_____

_____

Which pair of figures is congruent? _____

A. □ ▭

B. ◯ ◯

C.

D.

Ms. Silva's class collected 347 pounds of trash on clean-up day. Mr. Garcia's class collected 412 pounds of trash. How many more pounds of trash were collected by Mr. Garcia's class?

_____

```
  853
  227
  412
+ 337
```

Day # 2

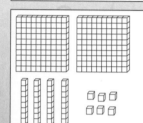

Use the model to show how to subtract 8 tens. What number is left?

_____

Use >, <, or = to compare.

8 x 3 ☐ 3 x 6

11 – 5 ☐ 3 x 2

8 x 5 ☐ 4 x 9

15 – 7 ☐ 11 – 8

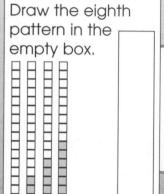

What time is shown on this clock?

_____

Draw the eighth pattern in the empty box.

Day # 3

Library	Number of Books
University	82,437
Children's	8,932
Archives	801,920
Historical	89,478

List the library sections in order from the least to the greatest number of books.

_____

_____

_____

_____

8 9 10 11 12 13 14 15

About how long is the nail?

○ 15 cm

○ 9 cm

○ 6 cm

○ 14 cm

222 224 226 228

What does this number line show?

○ the odd numbers between 200 and 230

○ the even numbers between 200 and 210

○ the even numbers between 220 and 230

```
  743
– 569
```

Day # 4

Student	Allowance
Tim	◯◯◯◯◯◯
Beth	◯◯◯
Sal	◯◯◯◯◯
Jake	◯◯◯◯

each ◯ 10¢

How much money was earned by all the students? _____

Elm Street is 5 blocks longer than Oak Street. Hickory Street is 3 blocks shorter than Pine Street. May Street is as long as Elm. To find out how long Hickory Street is, you need to know the length of which street?

○ Pine

○ Oak

○ May

Round each number to the nearest thousand.

8,153 → _____

2,512 → _____

983 → _____

6,710 → _____

Which shows the most accurate way to estimate the difference between 387 and 951?

○ 380 + 950

○ 1,000 – 400

○ 950 – 390

Name

Assessment

1
```
  125
  332
  798
+ 455
```

2
```
  531
- 184
```

3 Round each number to the nearest thousand.

5,672 → _____

881 → _____

7,199 → _____

4 Mr. Ortez's class read 538 books. Mr. Mile's class read 731 books. How many more books were read by Mr. Mile's class? Show your solution number sentence. _____

_____

_____

5 Use >, <, or = to compare.

7 x 4 ☐ 7 x 6

13 – 5 ☐ 4 x 2

8 x 4 ☐ 5 x 6

6

Program Name	Number of Graphics
Art Plus	56,120
Paintbrush	6,789
Colorific	65,882
Designs	556,022

List the CD-ROM names in order from the least number of graphics to the greatest number.

_____
_____
_____
_____

7 Write each number in expanded form.

572,486 _____

_____

325,147 _____

_____

8 Which pair of figures is congruent? _____

A.

B.

C.

D.

9 What time is shown on the clock? _____

10

Student	Number of Flowers Planted
Jenny	✻✻✻✻✻
Sarah	✻✻✻✻✻✻✻
Kiera	✻✻
Billy	✻✻✻✻✻✻✻✻

✻ = 5

What is the total number of flowers planted by the children?

_____ flowers

$300,000 + 40,000 + 6,000 + 100 + 50 + 2 =$

- ○ 34,652
- ○ 436,152
- ○ 346,152
- ○ 3,462

Which pair of figures is NOT congruent? _____

A.

B.

C.

D.

Deb's math book has 421 pages. Her spelling book has 276, and her science book has 352 pages. How many more pages does her math book have than her science book?

_____

8,850
− 2,472

Day #1

Use the model to show how to subtract 6 tens. What number is left? _____

$4 \times 3 = \boxed{} \times 6$

$25 - 5 = \boxed{} \times 4$

$6 \times 5 = 26 + \boxed{}$

To make $3.47, you would need

_____ dollar bills

_____ quarters

_____ dimes

_____ nickels

_____ pennies

Continue the pattern by writing the next three numbers.

25, 27, 30, 32, 35, 37, 40

_____ _____ _____

Day #2

Which is an even number that is less than 5,620 but more than 4,996?

- ○ 5,644
- ○ 5,328
- ○ 4,986
- ○ 6,248

What is the perimeter of a square that measures 8 inches on one side?

_____

---

531 533 535 537

This number line shows
- ○ the odd numbers between 530 and 538
- ○ the even numbers between 530 and 540
- ○ the odd numbers between 527 and 540

2,640
− 1,569

Day #3

Hen	Eggs Laid
Goldy	○○○○
Red	○○○○○○○
Sal	○○○○
Lulu	○○○○

each ○ = 20 eggs

Add symbols to the graph to show that Goldy laid 80 more eggs than Lulu.

In a horse race, Champ is 4 lengths ahead of Prince. Prince is 6 lengths behind Jetta. Star is 3 lengths ahead of Jetta. How many lengths is Champ behind Star? _____

What might be reasonable dimensions for the size of a kitchen?

- ○ 20 in. x 30 in.
- ○ 10 ft. x 14 ft.
- ○ 10 mi. x 14 mi.

Which shows the most accurate way to estimate the sum of 231 and 482?

- ○ 380 + 500
- ○ 400 + 300
- ○ 230 + 480

Day #4

Assessment

1

3,310
− 1,048

2

9,760
− 8,299

3 Continue the pattern by writing the next three numbers.

69, 74, 78, 83, 87, 92

_____ _____ _____

4

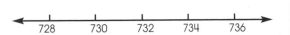

728   730   732   734   736

This number line shows

○ the even numbers between 730 and 740.

○ the even numbers between 726 and 738.

○ the odd numbers between 725 and 739.

5 Steve collected 741 stamps. Steve's grandfather collected 672 stamps. Steve's father collected 523 stamps. How many more stamps did Steve collect than his father? Show your solution in a number sentence.

_____

6

Student	Pages Read
Lilly	📖📖📖📖
Tad	📖📖
Bob	📖📖📖📖📖
Al	📖

📖 = 25 pages

Add symbols to the graph to show that Tad read 75 more pages than Al.

7 In a marathon race, Ben was 5 meters ahead of John. Frank was 12 meters ahead of Ben, and Sam was 4 meters behind Frank. How many meters ahead of John was Sam? _____

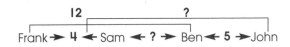

12   ?

Frank ► 4 ◄ Sam ◄ ? ► Ben ◄ 5 ► John

8 What is the perimeter of a square that measures 12 centimeters on one side?

_____

9 900,000 + 50,000 + 3,000 + 700 + 20 + 6 =

○ 95,372

○ 9,326

○ 935,726

○ 953,726

10 What might be reasonable dimensions for a bedroom?

○ 15 inches x 20 inches

○ 15 miles x 20 miles

○ 15 feet x 20 feet

What is the value of the 5 in each number?

Example:

3,**5**622   <u>5,000</u>

34,652   _____

436,125   _____

356,102   _____

3,562   _____

Match.

pentagon _____
quadrilateral _____
octagon _____
hexagon _____

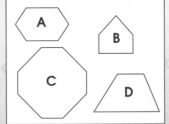

Joe scored 1,243 points on a video game. Matt's score was 1,458, and David's score was 985. Show how to find the difference between David's score and Joe's score.

_____

$$4,706 - 3,438$$

Day #1

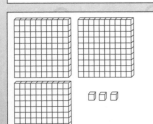

Use the model to show how to subtract 8 ones. What number is left? _____

---

8 x 3 =

(_____ x 3) + (_____ x 3)

7 x 4 =

(_____ x 4) + (_____ x 4)

9 x 6 =

(_____ x 6) + (_____ x 6)

To make $2.38 you would need

_____ dollar bills

_____ quarters

_____ dimes

_____ nickels

_____ pennies

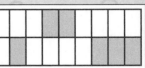

Continue the pattern by shading in the figure below.

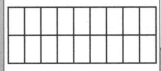

Day #2

Which is an odd number that is more than 7,821 but less than 10,000?

○ 9,340

○ 10,351

○ 1,975

○ 8,243

What is the perimeter of a rectangle that measures 27 inches on one side and 56 inches on the other side?

_____

97,435 is read

○ ninety thousand, four hundred three five

○ ninety-seven thousand, four hundred thirty-five

○ ninety-seven thousand, three hundred five

$$9,901 - 2,569$$

Day #3

Favorite Pizza

each △ = 2 votes

▨ cheese
■ pepperoni
□ bacon

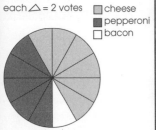

How many votes for pepperoni pizza? _____
cheese pizza? _____

A phone company wants to create some new area codes. Each new area code will have 3 numbers. Using the digits 1, 5, and 7 only once in each code, how many new codes can the phone company create?

_____ new area codes

About how many gallons of gasoline can a car hold?

○ 2 gallons

○ 20 gallons

○ 200 gallons

○ 2,000 gallons

| 4 | 7 | 3 | 4 | 2 |

These cards are shuffled and placed facedown after each turn. You draw 1 card, look at it, and return it to the deck. After drawing 10 times, you would probably draw a _____ most often.

Day #4

Assessment

1

$$9,402$$
$$- \ 1,027$$

2

$$5,705$$
$$- \ 2,299$$

3 About how many gallons of water would it take to fill the kitchen sink?

- ○ 3
- ○ 30
- ○ 300
- ○ 3,000

4 Rob, Sid, and Mark read 3 books each. The total number of pages Rob read was 2,134. Mark's total was 1,087, and Sid read a total of 876 pages. Show how to find the difference between the number of pages Sid read and the number of pages Rob read. _____

5

$$5 \times 7 = (\underline{\hspace{0.5cm}} \times 7) + (\underline{\hspace{0.5cm}} \times 7)$$

$$9 \times 4 = (\underline{\hspace{0.5cm}} \times 4) + (\underline{\hspace{0.5cm}} \times 4)$$

6 Which is an even number that is more than 8,234 but less than 9,933?

- ○ 8,328
- ○ 9,641
- ○ 9,944

7 What is the value of the 8 in each number?

85,231 _____

12,890 _____

8,725,231 _____

8 Match.

A   B

C   D

hexagon _____

pentagon _____

quadrilateral _____

octagon _____

9 To make $4.94, you would need

____ dollar bills

____ quarters

____ dimes

____ nickels

____ pennies

10 Use the model to show how to subtract 5 ones. What number is left? _____

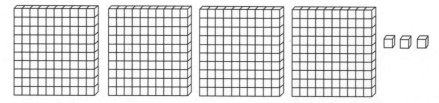

Day #1

What is the value of the 2 in each number?

Example: 35,620   <u>20</u>

234,651 _____

436,102 _____

2,356,109 _____

23,564 _____

By definition, which shape is a

pentagon _____
quadrilateral _____
octagon _____
hexagon _____

A.   **B.**

C.   **D.**

Lynn had $174. She spent $4 a week for 12 weeks for a total of $48. How much does Lynn have now?

_____

64,020
− 13,438

Day #2

Draw a base-ten model to show this number.

2,485

---

7 x 5 =

(_____ x 5) + (_____ x 5)

6 x 7 =

(_____ x 7) + (_____ x 7)

12 x 8 =

(_____ x 6) + (_____ x 6)

What time will this clock show in 15 minutes? _____

Continue the pattern by shading in the figure below.

Day #3

Which number would go in the empty box?

342, 344, [   ], 348

○ 351

○ 340

○ 345

○ 346

What is the perimeter of an octagon that measures 4 inches on each side?

_____

2,597,401 is read

○ two million, five hundred ninety-seven thousand, four hundred one

○ twenty-five thousand, five hundred nine, four hundred one

---

7 x 4 = _____

8 x 5 = _____

6 x 6 = _____

3 x 9 = _____

4 x 8 = _____

Day #4

Favorite Colors

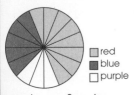

□ red
■ blue
□ purple

each △ = 3 votes

How many more votes for red than purple? _____

blue? _____

Using a red, blue, green, and yellow block only once in each row, how many four-block patterns can you make that have a red block in the first position?

_____ block patterns

* Bonus: How many patterns can be made in all?

About how long does it take to listen to a song?

○ 3 seconds

○ 3 minutes

○ 30 minutes

○ 3 hours

Shade in the spinner that would give you the best chance of landing on the number 3.

0-7682-3204-X *Math 4 Today*

Assessment

1

52,020
− 11,627

2

5 x 8 = _____

9 x 3 = _____

8 x 4 = _____

4 x 7 = _____

3 Continue the pattern by shading in the blank grid.

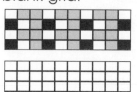

4 3,457,198 is read

○ three hundred fifty-seven million, one hundred ninety-eight

○ three million, four hundred fifty-seven thousand, one hundred ninety-eight

5 For the first 6 months of this year, Marcie watched 321 hours of TV. For the last 6 months, she watched 1 hour of TV a night for a total of 183 hours. How many more hours of TV did she watch during the first 6 months of the year?

_____

6 Which graph shows football having 20 more votes than baseball?_____
each △ = 5 votes

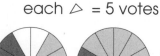

■ basketball
■ football
□ baseball

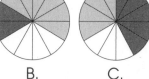

A.   B.   C.

7 What time will the clock show in 15 minutes? _____

8 What is the perimeter of a pentagon if each side measures 9 centimeters?

_____

9 What is the value of the 3 in each number?

83,467,109 _____

92,637,001 _____

157,472,139 _____

10 About how long does it take to brush your teeth?

○ 5 seconds

○ 180 seconds

○ 25 minutes

○ 3 hours

Which number has a digit of greater value in the tens place than in the thousands place?

○ 67,169

○ 82,505

○ 13,681

○ 21,910

Match.

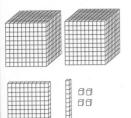

A. cylinder _____

B. rectangular prism _____

C. cube _____

D. triangular prism _____

Cindy was making floral arrangements for the Christmas banquet. She put 7 red carnations in each of 5 vases. Show how to find the number of carnations she used. _____

Subtract, then check by adding.

$$9,010 - 8,623$$

Day #1

Draw the missing pieces to make this base-ten model show 3,476.

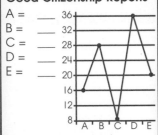

$2 \times (3 + 4) =$

$(2 \times 3) + (\underline{\quad} \times \underline{\quad})$

$5 \times (7 + 8) =$

$(5 \times 7) + (\underline{\quad} \times \underline{\quad})$

$4 \times (8 + 3) =$

$(4 \times 3) + (\underline{\quad} \times \underline{\quad})$

What time was shown on this clock 20 minutes ago? _____

Study the pattern on the cards below. What will the tenth card look like?

1	2	3	4
3	6	9	12

Day #2

Which number will go in the blank?

210, 200, _____, 180

○ 220

○ 190

○ 100

○ 205

What is the area of the figure below?

_____ square units

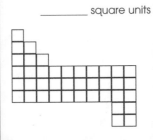

This number line shows

○ 12 − 12 = 0

○ 3 x 4 = 12

○ 7 + 5 = 12

○ 12 ÷ 2 = 6

---

7 x 3 = _____

6 x 5 = _____

8 x 2 = _____

9 x 4 = _____

4 x 7 = _____

Day #3

Good Citizenship Reports

A = _____
B = _____
C = _____
D = _____
E = _____

How many good citizenship reports were received by each class?

Marvin bought 8 party bags for his birthday guests. What information is needed in order to find out how much Marvin spent?

○ Marvin's age

○ the number of guests he invited

○ the cost of each party bag

○ the date of his birth

About how tall is a street delivery mailbox?

○ 3 kilometers

○ 3 meters

○ 3 centimeters

○ 3 kilograms

Shade in the spinner that would give you the best chance of landing on the number 1.

Day #4

Assessment

1

6,020
− 5,928

2

5 x 6 = _____

4 x 9 = _____

2 x 8 = _____

3 x 7 = _____

3 About how long is a school bus?

○ 10 millimeters

○ 10 centimeters

○ 10 meters

○ 10 kilometers

4 Jenna made 9 autumn collages. She used 4 leaves in each collage. How many leaves did Jenna use to make all her collages? _____

5

5 x (8 + 2) = (5 x 8) + (_____ x _____)

2 x (6 + 4) = (2 x 4) + (_____ x _____)

8 x (9 + 7) = (8 x 7) + (_____ x _____)

6 Which number goes in the empty box?

308, 304, 300, [   ] , 292

○ 302

○ 290

○ 310

○ 296

7 Which number has a digit of greater value in the ten thousands place than in the millions place?

○ 25,431,207

○ 147,358,110

○ 4,129,782

○ 43,847,208

8 Match.

_____ rectangular prism   _____ cube

_____ cylinder   _____ triangular prism

A.   B.   C.   D.

9

What time was shown on this clock 25 minutes ago? _____

10 This number line shows

○ 6 x 3 = 18

○ 18 ÷ 2 = 9

○ 6 + 6 = 12

○ 18 − 12 = 6

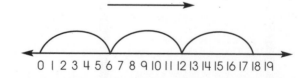

0 1 2 3 4 5 6 7 8 9 10 11 12 13 14 15 16 17 18 19

Day #1

Which number has a digit of lesser value in the ten thousands place than in the ten millions place?

○ 11,247,169

○ 891,250,505

○ 138,681,456

○ 201,910,872

Which shape has a line of symmetry?

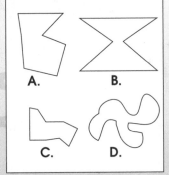

A.   B.

C.   D.

Ray ordered pizza for 9 of his friends. In order for each of his friends to have 4 pieces of pizza, how many pieces of pizza did Ray need to order? _____

Subtract. Check by adding.

5,000
– 2,716

Day #2

Write the fraction for the shaded part of each shape.

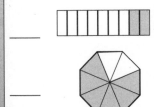

___

___

8 x (5 + 2) =

(____ x ____) +

(____ x ____)

= ☐

or

8 x ____ = ☐

Using a minimal collection of coins (the least amount possible), show how to make $1.17.

_____

_____

Study the pattern on the cards below. What will the tenth card look like?

1	2	3	4
7	14	21	28

tenth →
card

Day #3

Which number is 100 less than 2,458?

○ 2,258

○ 2,558

○ 1,458

○ 2,358

What is the area of the figure below?

_____ sq. cm

8 cm

6 cm

0 1 2 3 4 5 6 7 8 9 10 11 12 13 14 15

This number line shows

○ 5 x 3 = 15

○ 4 x 3 = 12

○ 7 + 8 = 15

○ 10 ÷ 2 = 5

7 x 6 = _____

9 x 5 = _____

8 x 8 = _____

6 x 3 = _____

7 x 7 = _____

Day #4

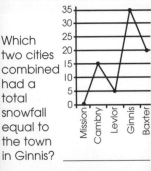

Yearly Snowfall
snowfall measured in inches

Which two cities combined had a total snowfall equal to the town in Ginnis? _____

_____

Todd swam 7 laps a day last summer. Phil swam 5 laps every 3 days. What information do you need to find out the total number of laps that Todd swam last summer?

○ the distance Todd swam each day

○ the number of days Phil swam

○ the number of days Todd swam

Estimate the sum by rounding to the hundreds place.

587
217
620
+ 188

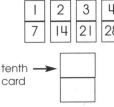

The marbles above are in a sack. With one draw, the chances are 1 out of 7 that you could draw a ◯. What would be the probability of drawing a ●?

_____ out of _____

Assessment

1

8,000
− 2,817

2

3 x 6 = _____

5 x 9 = _____

8 x 8 = _____

6 x 7 = _____

3

If the above tiles are placed in a box, what are the chances of drawing a ☐ on the first draw?

_____ out of _____

4

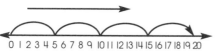

0 1 2 3 4 5 6 7 8 9 10 11 12 13 14 15 16 17 18 19 20

This number line shows

○ 20 − 20 = 0   ○ 20 ÷ 4 = 5

○ 11 + 9 = 20   ○ 5 x 4 = 20

5 Amy bought gifts for her 7 cousins. Each gift cost $4.00. How much money did Amy spend for all the gifts?

_____

6 **Class President Election**

Which two students' combined votes equal the same number of votes Pam received?

_____

_____

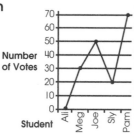

Number of Votes
70
60
50
40
30
20
10
0

Ali Meg Joe Sly Pam

Student

7 Using a minimal collection of coins (the least amount possible), show how to make $1.38.

_____

8 Find the area.

_____ sq. cm

9 cm

4 cm

9 Which number has a digit of lesser value in the hundred millions place than in the thousands place?

○ 457,126,990

○ 825,992,132

○ 175,071,976

○ 239,190,843

10 Estimate the sum by rounding to the hundreds place.

781
411
652
+ 293

How many digits are needed to create a number in the

hundred millions? _____

ten thousands? ____

hundreds? _____

Which shape has two lines of symmetry? _____

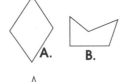

A.   B.

C.   D.

Hannah completed 4 pages of homework every day for 7 days. How many pages of homework did she complete in all? _____

Subtract. Check by adding.

$$\begin{array}{r} 3,000 \\ -\ 2,971 \\ \hline \end{array}$$

Write the fraction for the shaded parts of each shape.

 _____

 _____

$5 \times (8 + 2) =$

$(5 \times 8) + (5 \times$ ____ $)$

$=$ ☐

$3 \times (7 + 1) =$

$(3 \times 7) + (3 \times$ ____ $)$

$=$ ☐

Using a minimal number of the coins below (the least amount possible), show how to make $1.74.

____ quarters ____ dimes

____ nickels ____ pennies

31, 28, 25, 22

The formula for the pattern above is

○ add 3

○ subtract 3

○ count by 5s

○ subtract 2

What number is 1,000 more than 9,235?

○ 9,335

○ 8,235

○ 10,235

○ 11,235

What is the perimeter of the figure below?

____ units

What is the area?

____ square units

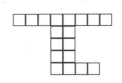

Write the number word for

2,000,405 _____

_____

_____

610,240 _____

_____

_____

$9 \times 8 =$ _____

$8 \times 7 =$ _____

$7 \times 6 =$ _____

$9 \times 7 =$ _____

$8 \times 4 =$ _____

Use >, < , or = to describe the information in this graph.

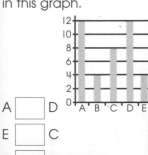

A ☐ D

E ☐ C

D ☐ B

Mystery Numbers

A = B x 3

B = D – 10

C = the sum of 7 and 3

D = C + C

A = _____

B = _____

C = _____

D = _____

Estimate the sum by rounding to the tens place.

$$\begin{array}{r} 2,832 \\ 1,179 \\ 6,208 \\ +\ 4,385 \\ \hline \end{array}$$

● ▲ ▲ ▲ ▲ ■ ■

The above shapes are in a sack. With one draw, the chance of drawing a ▲ would be

____ out of ____

Assessment

1 Subtract. Check by adding.

$$\begin{array}{r} 7,000 \\ -\ 6,294 \\ \hline \end{array}$$

2

6 x 7 = _____

8 x 9 = _____

4 x 8 = _____

7 x 8 = _____

3 Estimate the sum by rounding to the tens place.

$$\begin{array}{r} 4,351 \\ 4,174 \\ 3,233 \\ +\ 5,155 \\ \hline \end{array}$$

4 Nate was at summer camp for 9 days. He went fishing each day. If he caught 6 fish every time he went fishing, how many fish did he catch while he was at camp? _____

5

6 x (4 + 5) = (6 x 4) + (6 x _____) = ☐

5 x (2 + 7) = (5 x 2) + (5 x _____) = ☐

6 Which number is 1,000 less than 10,247?

○ 9,247

○ 11,237

○ 10,357

○ 9,147

7 How many digits are needed to create a number in the

hundred thousands_____

ten millions _____

thousands _____

8 Which figure has two lines of symmetry? _____

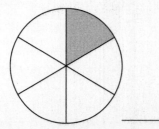

A.   B.   C.

9 Using a minimal collection of the coins below, show how to make $2.49.

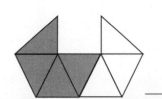

_____ _____ _____ _____
quarters   dimes   nickels   pennies

10 Write the fraction for the shaded part of each figure.

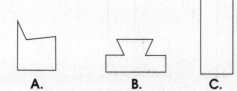

_____   _____   _____

Write the number with the following place values.

eight ten thousands, five hundreds, two tens, seven ones

_____

Shade the figures that have dotted lines showing the lines of symmetry.

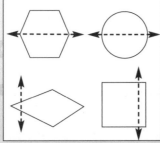

Mr. Know has 24 students in his science class. He would like to have 4 students at each table. How many tables will he need for his class?

_____

---

9 x 9 = _____

8 x 8 = _____

7 x 7 = _____

6 x 6 = _____

5 x 5 = _____

Day #1

Write the equivalent fractions.

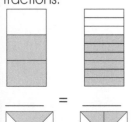

_____ = _____

Write the fact family for 7, 8, and 56.

_____

_____

_____

_____

Kim began her piano practice at 4:20. She practiced for 35 minutes. At what time did she stop practicing?

_____

Which equation describes the pattern?

○ n + n

○ n x n

○ n – n

○ n + 2

Day #2

Which number is less than 11,437 and more than 10,992?

○ 10,990

○ 11,532

○ 10,005

○ 11,235

What is the perimeter of the figure below?

_____ cm

What is the area?

_____ sq. cm

9 cm

5 cm

Write the number words.

15,320,100 _____

_____

_____

350,205,500 _____

_____

_____

---

16 ÷ 2 = _____

25 ÷ 5 = _____

8 ÷ 4 = _____

12 ÷ 3 = _____

15 ÷ 3 = _____

Day #3

Gymnastic Meet Total Scores

Christy	35
Alicia	40
Leyla	25
Kalyn	50

On the back of this paper, draw a bar graph to describe the data in the chart with 1 bar = 5. Write three summary statements.

Mystery Numbers

A = B x 7

B = 12 ÷ 3

C = D – A

D = A + B

A = _____ B = _____

C = _____ D = _____

Dennis bought a game for $27.50, a book for $6.25, a model kit for $14.95, and a shirt for $22.99. About how much money did he spend?

○ $71.00

○ $85.00

○ $100.00

○ $92.00

Match.

_____ 10 centimeters

_____ 100 centimeters

_____ 10 decimeters

_____ 1,000 meters

A. kilometer

B. meter

C. decimeter

Day #4

Assessment

1

16 ÷ 8 = _____

18 ÷ 2 = _____

25 ÷ 5 = _____

15 ÷ 3 = _____

2

6 x 6 = _____

8 x 8 = _____

4 x 4 = _____

9 x 9 = _____

3

20	18	16	14
10	9	8	7

The equation for this pattern is

○ even n + 5

○ even n – 4

○ even n ÷ 2

4 Write each number word.

251,718,400 _____

_____

_____

62,502,194 _____

_____

_____

5 Kala has 35 stickers to give to each of her 5 friends. How many stickers will she give each friend if each one gets the same number of stickers?

_____

6

100s on the Spelling Tests

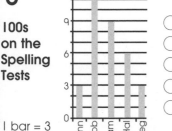

1 bar = 3

Which statements are true for this graph?

○ Bob > Meg

○ Hal > Sam

○ Meg = Ann

○ Sam = 9

○ Ann + Meg + Hal = Bob

7 Margo and Patsy went to see a play. The play began at 3:20 and lasted for 45 minutes. At what time did the play end? _____

8 What is the perimeter of the figure?

_____ cm

What is the area?

_____ sq. cm

7 cm

4 cm

9 Write the number made up of each of the following place values.

eighty millions, four hundred-thousands, two hundreds, nine tens, five ones

_____

_____

10 Heidi was doing chores to earn money. She earned $7.54 during the first week of November. She earned $32.99 during the second week, $12.50 the third week, and $24.95 the last week of the month. About how much money did Heidi earn during November?

○ $100.00

○ $85.00

○ $66.00

○ $79.00

Day #1

Fill in the missing digits.

seven hundred sixty-two million, nine hundred forty-five thousand, two hundred fifty-eight

7___2,___ ___5,___ ___8

Match.

line XY _____

line segment XY ___

ray XY _____

1.
2.
3.

Ms. Rye has 12 roses, 18 daisies, and 3 vases. She wants an equal number of roses and an equal number of daisies in each vase. Show how to find the number of roses and daisies she will put in each vase.

_____

---

9 x 6 = _____

8 x 5 = _____

9 x 8 = _____

8 x 7 = _____

9 x 4 = _____

Day #2

Shade in the second figure in each pair to complete the equivalent fractions. Fill in the second fraction.

 $\frac{1}{2}$ = ____

 = ____

 ____ = ____

Which pair are NOT related facts?

○ 8 x 9 = 72
  72 ÷ 9 = 8

○ 6 x 6 = 36
  6 – 6 = 0

○ 8 x 4 = 32
  4 x 8 = 32

○ 7 x 5 = 35
  35 ÷ 5 = 7

The Hampton family arrived at their grandparents' home at 6:40 Sunday evening. The drive had taken 1 hour and 10 minutes. At what time did the Hamptons leave home? _____

1, 6, 4, 9, 7, 12, 10, 15, 13, 18, 16, 21

What is the rule for the above pattern?

_____

_____

Day #3

Which number is more than 125,437, but less then 220,151?

○ 110,790

○ 251,031

○ 100,005

○ 211,835

What is the perimeter of the figure below?

_____ units

What is the area?

_____ square units

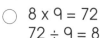
0 1 2 3 4 5 6 7 8 9 10 11 12 13 14 15

This number line shows

○ 14 – 9 = 5

○ 7 + 8 = 15

○ 14 ÷ 7 = 2

○ 7 x 7 = 49

---

18 ÷ 3 = _____

24 ÷ 6 = _____

27 ÷ 9 = _____

36 ÷ 6 = _____

20 ÷ 4 = _____

Day #4

Student Spelling Stars

Kira	★★★★★
Mike	★★★
Lance	★★★★★★
Deb	★

each ★ = 6 A+ tests

What is the total number of A+ spelling tests shown on this graph? _____

Max is older than Ivan. Hal is younger than Ivan but older than Greg.

Which statements could be true?

○ Max is older than Hal.

○ Ivan is younger than Greg.

○ Hal is the youngest.

○ Greg is younger than Max.

Quaid picked 82 bushels of apples on Monday and 91 bushels on Tuesday. Carmen picked 52 bushels on Wednesday and 75 bushels on Thursday. About how many more bushels of apples did Quaid pick?

○ 70   ○ 40

○ 20   ○ 100

---

10 centimeters = 1 decimeter

It takes 8 decimeters of shipping paper to wrap a large package for mailing. How many centimeters of paper would be needed?

_____

Assessment

1

20 ÷ 5 = _____

18 ÷ 6 = _____

24 ÷ 4 = _____

27 ÷ 3 = _____

2

4 x 9 = _____

7 x 8 = _____

8 x 9 = _____

6 x 9 = _____

3 Eva read 22 pages on Monday and 91 pages on Tuesday. Mario read 89 pages on Monday and 63 pages on Tuesday. About how many more pages did Mario read?

○ 20   ○ 50

○ 40   ○ 90

4 Juan has 42 stamps and 36 stickers. He wants to glue the same number of stamps and the same number of stickers onto 6 pages in his collector's album. Show how to find the total number of stamps and stickers he will put on each page.

_____

5 Which pair are NOT related facts?

○ 8 x 8 = 64   64 ÷ 8 = 8

○ 8 + 8 = 16   8 – 8 = 0

○ 4 x 6 = 24   6 x 4 = 24

○ 5 x 9 = 45   45 ÷ 9 = 5

6 Which numbers are more than 347,129 but less than 412,076?

○ 418,000   ○ 398,899

○ 409,778   ○ 362,901

○ 447,202   ○ 332,388

○ 4,001,033   ○ 34,100

7 Fill in the missing digits for each number.

nine hundred eighty-six thousand, four hundred thirty-five

9___ ___,___3___

8 Match.

____ line AB

____ ray AB

____ line segment AB

____ ray YX

____ line segment XY

A. X———————Y

B. A⟷———————B

C. X⟵———————Y

D. A———————B⟶

E. A———————B

9 A new play is opening in the city. It begins at 8:00. It takes Carol's family 1 hour and 25 minutes to drive to the city. At what time should Carol's family leave home in order to arrive at the play on time? _____

10 Shade in the second figure to complete the equivalent fraction.

 ___ = ___   ___ = ___

Day #1

Write in expanded form.

two hundred ninety-one thousand, eight hundred fifteen

_____

_____

Match.
A. ray   B. line
C. line segment

_____ a straight figure with two end points

_____ a straight figure, with no end points, that extends forever in both directions

_____ a straight figure, with one end point, that extends forever in one direction

---

Holly displays her 54 music boxes on 6 shelves in her room. She also keeps 12 dolls on the shelves. If she arranges the music boxes and the dolls equally, how many items are on each shelf? _____

$$34 \times 2 \qquad 43 \times 3$$

$$51 \times 5 \qquad 52 \times 4$$

Day #2

Shade in the second figure to complete the equivalent fraction.

 =

_____   _____

 =

_____   _____

A common factor of 4 and 8 is 2 because 2 x 2 = 4 and 2 x 4 = 8.

Other than 1, what is a common factor for these number pairs?

10 and 15 _____

12 and 21 _____

7 and 14 _____

Name the amount needed for change.

Cost   Amount Given
$0.79 $1.00
Change _____

Cost   Amount Given
$0.37 $0.50
Change _____

2, 4, 7, 14, 17, 34, 37, 74, 77, 154

What is the rule for the pattern?

_____

_____

Day #3

Mountain	Feet in Height
Annapuma	26,504
Kilimanjaro	19,340
Dap Sang	28,250
Everest	29,028
Cho Oyu	26,750

List the mountains in order of height from least to greatest.

_____

_____

_____

_____

_____

What is perimeter of the figure below?

_____ units
What is the area?

_____ square units

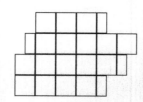

0 1 2 3 4 5 6 7 8 9 10 11 12 13 14 15

This number line shows

○ 15 ÷ 5 = 3

○ 7 + 8 = 15

○ 5 ÷ 5 = 1

○ 5 x 5 = 25

---

49 ÷ 7 = _____

54 ÷ 6 = _____

63 ÷ 9 = _____

72 ÷ 8 = _____

81 ÷ 9 = _____

Day #4

Hours of TV Watched per Month

Room 401 ☐☐

Room 402 ☐☐☐☐

Room 403 ☐☐☐☐☐

each ☐ = 25 hours

How many more hours of TV were watched by Room 403 than Room 401? _____

Ann read fewer books than Susan. Linda read more books than Ann, but fewer than Tammy. Which statements could be true?

○ Ann read the least number of books.

○ Tammy read the most.

○ Linda read more books than Tammy.

Todd earned the following amounts last summer.

June	$57.98
July	$92.33
August	$66.88

About how much money did Todd earn last summer?

○ $220   ○ $250

○ $300   ○ $120

---

10 decimeters = 1 meter

Sam measured 8 meters to make a pen for his pet rabbits. At the store, the fencing he wanted for the pen was sold only in decimeters. How many decimeters of fencing would he need to buy? _____

Name _____

Assessment

1

$63 \div 7 =$ _____

$72 \div 9 =$ _____

$54 \div 9 =$ _____

$49 \div 7 =$ _____

2

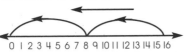

$\begin{array}{c} 43 \\ \times\ 2 \end{array}$ $\begin{array}{c} 63 \\ \times\ 3 \end{array}$ $\begin{array}{c} 12 \\ \times\ 4 \end{array}$

3 What is the rule for this pattern?

1, 3, 2, 6, 5, 15, 14, 42, 41

_____

4

0 1 2 3 4 5 6 7 8 9 10 11 12 13 14 15 16

This number line shows

○ $8 + 8 = 16$ ○ $16 \div 2 = 8$

○ $8 \times 8 = 64$ ○ $8 - 8 = 0$

5 Marcus is setting the table for his party. He has invited 8 guests. For party favors, he bought 24 balloons and 16 candy bars. How many party favors will he set at each place if each guest gets an equal number of balloons and candy bars? _____

6 **Students Wearing Glasses**   each b = 30 students

A. Grade _____

Third	bbbb
Fourth	bbb
Fifth	bbbbbb
Sixth	bbbbb

B. Grade _____

Third	bbb
Fourth	bbbbbb
Fifth	bbbbbbb
Sixth	b

Which graph shows that 90 more students in fifth grade wear glasses than the students in fourth grade? _____

7 Name the coins and amounts needed for change

Cost $5.49   Amount Given $6.00

_____

_____

Cost $3.22   Amount Given $4.12

_____

_____

8 What is the perimeter and the area of the figure below?

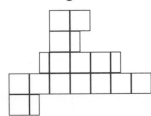

perimeter = _____ units

area = _____ square units

9 Write each number in expanded form.

fifty-seven thousand, three hundred eighty-one _____

_____

10 The chart shows the number of long distance calls made by the School Computer Supply Company for the fall months of 2002.

Month	Number of Calls
September	297
October	341
November	196

About how many calls were made by the company during these months?

○ 700   ○ 900

○ 600   ○ 800

Day #1

$400,000 + 90,000 + 3,000 + 500 + 7 =$

○ forty-nine thousand, three hundred fifty-seven

○ four hundred nine thousand, three thousand seven

○ four hundred ninety-three thousand, five hundred seven

Which show right angles?

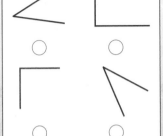

○   ○

○   ○

James is making collages for his 4 aunts. For decoration, he wants to put 6 leaves, 4 shells, and 3 flowers on each collage. How many decorations will he need to make all the collages?

_____

_____

$\begin{array}{r} 44 \\ \times\ 5 \\ \hline \end{array}$ $\begin{array}{r} 13 \\ \times\ 7 \\ \hline \end{array}$

$\begin{array}{r} 58 \\ \times\ 5 \\ \hline \end{array}$ $\begin{array}{r} 29 \\ \times\ 4 \\ \hline \end{array}$

Day #2

Shade in $\frac{1}{3}$ of each set.

☐☐☐
☐☐☐

○○○○○○
○○○○○○
○○○○○○

A common factor of 4 and 8 is 2 because 2 x 2 = 4 and 2 x 4 = 8.

Other than 1, what is a common factor for these number pairs?

27 and 18 _____

30 and 40 _____

35 and 21 _____

Name the bills, coins, and amount needed for change.

Cost   **Amount Given**
$3.81 $5.00

Change _____

_____

Cost   **Amount Given**
$7.17 $10.00

Change _____

_____

Continue the pattern.

45	42	39	36
15	14	13	12

33		
11		

Day #3

Write the odd numbers between 3,497 and 3,511.

_____

_____

_____

_____

_____

Mrs. Thomas drove from Dallas, Texas to Ft. Worth, Texas. She traveled about

○ 55 kilograms

○ 55 liters

○ 55 kilometers

○ 55 decimeters

Write AM or PM.

Julio's party begins at 3:00. _____

The school tardy bell rings at 8:15. _____

The toy store opens at 9:30. _____

The evening news comes on at 6:00. ____

$9 \times \underline{\hspace{1cm}} = 72$

$3 \times \underline{\hspace{1cm}} = 27$

$\underline{\hspace{1cm}} \times 4 = 32$

$\underline{\hspace{1cm}} \times 7 = 63$

Day #4

School	Solar System Projects
Dayton	★★★★✦
Ryan	★★★
Adly	★★★★★✦
Marcus	★✦

each ★ = 4

How many solar system projects were entered in the science fair? _____

Tyesha and Eric together have 29 posters. Eric has 7 more posters than Tyesha. How many posters does each student have?

_____

Estimate the differences by rounding to the hundreds place.

$\begin{array}{r} 2,359 \\ -\ 1,231 \\ \hline \end{array}$ $\begin{array}{r} 7,944 \\ -\ 5,679 \\ \hline \end{array}$

1,000 meters = 1 kilometer

Tam and Isaac walked $2\frac{1}{2}$ kilometers along a hiking trail. How many meters did they walk? _____

Assessment

1

$9 \times \underline{\hspace{1cm}} = 63$

$8 \times \underline{\hspace{1cm}} = 32$

$\underline{\hspace{1cm}} \times 9 = 27$

$\underline{\hspace{1cm}} \times 9 = 72$

2

29	38	69
× 2	× 4	× 3

3 Estimate the difference by rounding to the hundreds place.

$$8,712$$
$$- 4,189$$

4 Mrs. Wong is making centerpieces for 7 tables. She wants to put 8 daisies, 7 carnations, and 5 roses in each centerpiece. How many flowers will she need? _____

5 What is a common factor for each pair of numbers?

45 and 10 _____

81 and 72 _____

36 and 30 _____

6 Write the even numbers between 5,996 and 6,010.

_____   _____

_____   _____

_____   _____

7 $600,000 + 70,000 + 2,000 + 10 + 4 =$

○ six hundred seventy-two thousand, fourteen

○ six hundred seven thousand, two hundred fourteen

○ sixty-seven million, two thousand, one hundred four

8 Lilly's family left home from Dallas, Texas for a ski trip in Denver, Colorado. About how far did they travel?

○ 1,200 grams

○ 1,200 centimeters

○ 1,200 kilometers

○ 1,200 meters

9 Write AM or PM.

Raul's parents went to a late movie. They returned home at 11:30. _____

Cindy had a piano lesson after school. Her lesson started at 4:30. _____

Gerald's dad took an early flight. His plane left at 7:30. _____

10 Shade in $\frac{1}{5}$ of each set.

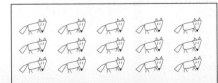

Name

Day #1

What is the value of the 5 in each number?

3,458,201 _____

152,670,400 _____

61,250 _____

Which show acute angles?

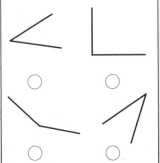

○   ○

○   ○

At Midland Elementary, there are 22 students in each of 7 fourth-grade classes. How many students are in fourth-grade at Midland? _____

```
  17        23
x 10      x 10


  84        33
x 10      x 10
```

Day #2

Shade in $\frac{2}{6}$ of each set.

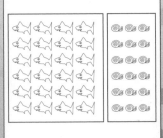

Other than 1, what are the common factors for these number pairs?

24 and 12 _____

_____

10 and 30 _____

_____

What time will the clock show in 2 hours and 15 minutes? _____

What figure would come next in this pattern?

○

Day #3

145,298 ☐ ☐ 167,109

Which two numbers could go in the empty boxes?

○ 168,231   169,345

○ 142,789   234,188

○ 14,388   15,632

○ 156,954   162,599

Mr. Valdez was loading stones to put into a wheelbarrow. The wheelbarrow can carry the weight of about

○ 80 grams

○ 80 kilograms

○ 80 kilometers

○ 80 centimeters

Write the number using numerals for seven hundred eighty-six million, four hundred two thousand, five hundred ninety-one

_____

```
 100       100
x 15      x 46


 100       100
x 72      x 93
```

Day #4

What is the difference between the number of points scored by Mark and the number of points scored by Hank? _____

Volleyball Tournament Points

Judy and Ramey together have 42 stuffed animals. Judy has 12 fewer animals than Ramey. How many stuffed animals does each girl have? _____

_____

Lynn's Reading Chart

Monday	36 pages
Tuesday	42 pages
Wednesday	39 pages
Thursday	0 pages

How could you estimate the total number of pages Lynn read?

○ 42 ÷ 4   ○ 40 x 3

○ 42 – 39   ○ 20 x 4

In a deck of 52 cards, there are 2 jokers and 4 each of the number cards 1–10. The probability of picking a joker is 2 out of 52 or $\frac{2}{52}$. Write, as a fraction, the probability of drawing a number 7 card.

_____

Assessment

1

$$85 \\ \times 10$$ $$79 \\ \times 10$$

2

$$100 \\ \times 51$$ $$100 \\ \times 62$$

3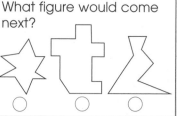

What figure would come next?

○   ○   ○

4 Write each number.

seventy-nine million, three hundred twenty-nine thousand, five hundred forty _____

four hundred ten million, three thousand, one hundred eighty-two

_____

5 There are 9 photographs on each page of a travel book. The book has 67 pages. How many photographs are in the book? _____

6 What is the difference between the pounds of paper recycled by Max and the pounds of paper recycled by Lou? _____

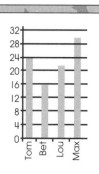

7 In art class, Kaly and Nate together painted 33 pictures during the year. Kaly painted 9 fewer pictures than Nate. How many pictures did each child paint? _____

8 Label each angle.

RA = right angle   AA = acute angle

< ∨ < ∨ ∟

___ ___ ___ ___ ___

9 What is the value of the 3 in each number?

321,890,267 _____

889,032,901 _____

3,290,177,200 _____

10

Basketball Goals for the Season	
Ty	17
Jamal	23
Pete	24
Kito	2
Nino	21

How could you estimate the number of goals made by all the boys?

○ 23 + 24 + 17

○ 4 x 20

○ 5 x 20

○ 5 x 25

○ 25 – 5

Day #1

What is the value of the 2 in each number?

9,468,201 _____

752,610,400 _____

21,390 _____

Which show obtuse angles?

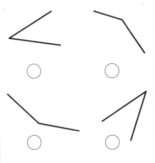

○   ○

○   ○

If there are 365 days in one year, how many days are in 7 years?

_____

```
   37
 x 30
_____
```

```
   54
 x 40
_____
```

Day #2

$\frac{1}{6}$ of 48 = _____

$\frac{1}{8}$ of 40 = _____

$\frac{1}{2}$ of 10 = _____

List the common factors for these number pairs. Circle the greatest common factor for each pair.

40 and 8 _____

_____

36 and 24 _____

_____

What time did the clock show 2 hours and 20 minutes ago? _____

Draw the sixth box in this pattern.

⇧ ⇩ ⇦ ⇨

⇧ ⇩ ⇦ ⇨
⇧ ⇩ ⇦ ⇨

⇧ ⇩ ⇦ ⇨
⇧ ⇩ ⇦ ⇨
⇧ ⇩ ⇦ ⇨

Day #3

100,051 ☐ ☐ 99,109

Which two numbers could go in the empty boxes?

○ 105,231   109,345

○ 906,789   902,188

○ 99,838   99,632

○ 98,054   93,107

Sandy made a jug of lemonade to serve 5 friends. About how much lemonade did she make?

○ 3 meters

○ 3 grams

○ 3 liters

○ 3 milliliters

Write each number.

six million, twenty-two thousand, four hundred eighty-seven

_____

twenty-five million, three hundred seventeen thousand, fifty-nine

_____

```
  357        652
x   8      x   7
```

```
  229        934
x   5      x   3
```

Day #4

Write each number pair.

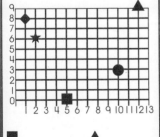

■ _____   ▲ _____

◆ _____   ● _____

★ _____

Mother needs to buy paper cups for 42 people. Which 2 packages could she buy to have enough paper cups without too many left over?

____ and ____

10	15	20	25
A	B	C	D

Four hundred seventy-two people bought concert tickets for $21.05 each. Which would be a way to estimate how much money was paid for the tickets?

○ 400 x $20 = $8,000

○ 500 x $20 = $10,000

○ 470 + $20 = $4970

○ 500 - $25 = $475

●●○○○○○

If these marbles are placed in a bag and one is drawn out, what is the probability that it will be white? _____

What is the probability that it will be black? _____

Assessment

1

95	62
x 50	x 80

2

498	873
x 7	x 7

3 While on vacation, the Carter family drove 337 miles a day for 16 days. How could you estimate the number of miles they drove?

○ 300 x 20 = 6,000
○ 400 x 20 = 8,000
○ 337 – 16 = 321
○ 300 + 20 = 320

4 There are 168 hours in 1 week. How many hours are in 9 weeks?

_____

5 List the common factors for these number pairs. Circle the greatest common factor.

64 and 16   _____

40 and 8   _____

6 Which two numbers could go in the empty boxes?

103,032 ☐ ☐ 100,091

○ 101,977   99,090
○ 104,234   100,459
○ 99,821   98,305
○ 100,621   100,243

7 What is the value of the 9 in each number?

391,820,267_____

889,032,501_____

3,270,179,200_____

8 Label the angles.
RA = right angle AA = acute angle
OA = obtuse angle

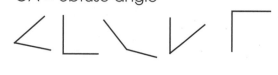

___ ___ ___ ___ ___

9 What time did the clock show 4 hours and 20 minutes ago? _____

10

$\frac{1}{7}$ of 49 = _____

$\frac{1}{4}$ of 20 = _____

$\frac{1}{9}$ of 36 = _____

Which number shows 7 thousands, 4 hundreds, 6 tens, and 18 ones?

- ○ 76,418
- ○ 74,618
- ○ 7,478

Which figures are polygons?

○   ○

○   ○

Marly's Country Store has 20 gumdrops in each of 6 candy jars. Which method could be used to find the total number of gumdrops?

- ○ add 20 and 6
- ○ multiply 20 by 6
- ○ subtract 6 from 20
- ○ divide 20 by 6

$$500 \times 28 \qquad 300 \times 56$$

$\frac{1}{5}$ of 25 = _____

$\frac{1}{3}$ of 33 = _____

$\frac{1}{7}$ of 56 = _____

A. sum   B. difference
C. quotient D. product

_____ the answer to a division problem

_____ the answer to an addition problem

_____ the answer to a subtraction problem

_____ the answer to a multiplication problem

Kyle bought 6 new model kits. Each kit cost $8.79. How much money did Kyle spend on model kits?

_____

XXXXXXXXXX
XXXXXXXXXX
X XXXXXXXX
XXXXXXXXXX
X X XXXXXX
XXXXXXXXXX
X X X XXXX
XXXXXXXXXX

How many Xs will be in the tenth box? _____

President	Term Served
Harry Truman	1945–1953
James Monroe	1817–1825
John Tyler	1841–1845
Herbert Hoover	1929–1933
John Adams	1797–1801

List the Presidents in order beginning with the earliest term to the most recent. _____

_____
_____
_____
_____

A.   9 kilograms
B.   3 meters
C.   2 grams
D.   300 liters
E.   20 milliliters
F.   1,500 kilograms
G.   80 kilograms

Which is the best estimate of mass for

car _____

sack of groceries _____

pencil_____

TV _____

Which number line shows the whole numbers that are greater than 4 and less than 10? _____

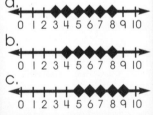

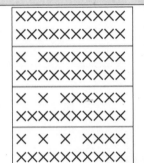

3)14

5)19

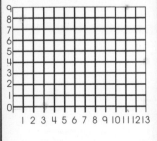

Plot these number pairs.

(11, 9)   (3, 0)

(13, 4)   (1, 8)

To decorate 5 dozen cupcakes with red hot candies, Nan needs about 550 red hots. Which 2 sacks of candy would be the best buy? _____

_____

353   177   255   379

Nine hundred thirty-seven people are seated at 28 tables for a banquet. How could you find the best estimate of the number of people at each table?

- ◉ 900 ÷ 30 = 30
- ○ 900 x 20 = 18,000
- ○ 1,000 – 28 = 972
- ○ 1,000 ÷ 20 = 50

●●○○◉○○○

If these marbles are placed in a bag and one is drawn out, what is the probability that it will be white or black?

_____

Assessment

1

900	600
x 13	x 72

2

$4\overline{)27}$ $8\overline{)70}$

3

□□□○○○○◆

If these shapes are in a bag, what is the probability (expressed as a fraction) of drawing out a ◆ or a □?

_____

4 Which number line shows the numbers that are less than 12 and more than 5? _____

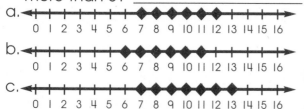

a.
b.
c.

5 Zeke packs 45 cans in each box. Today he packed 35 boxes. What method could be used to find the number of cans Zeke packed today?

○ add 45 and 35

○ multiply 45 by 35

○ subtract 35 from 45

6 Graph the number pairs.

(9, 11)

(3, 6)

(0, 10)

(7, 5)

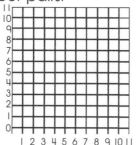

7 Ms. Silva needs to buy napkins for her company's picnic. She needs 715 napkins. Which 2 packages would be the best buy?

_____ and _____

256   395   125   500

8 What is the best estimate of mass for

a pumpkin _____   a bus _____

a football _____   a spoon _____

A. 2,000 kilograms   B. 2,000 kilometers

C. 10 grams   D. 10 liters

E. 15 meters   F. 15 kilograms

G. 2 milliliters   H. 2 kilograms

9 Which number shows 56 thousands, 2 hundreds, 37 tens, and 8 ones?

○ 562,378

○ 56,378

○ 56,578

○ 56,478

10 Eight hundred fifteen new compact disks arrived at the music store. The disks are put on display racks in groups of 52. How could you find the best estimate of the number of display racks needed for the compact disks?

○ 800 x 50 = 40,000

○ 900 x 60 = 54,000

○ 800 + 50 = 850

○ 800 ÷ 50 = 16

Day #1

Which number shows 8 thousands, 4 hundreds, 11 tens, and 6 ones?

○ 8,411

○ 8,516

○ 9,116

Which letter is inside the square and circle but not inside the rectangle? _____

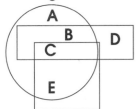

Hannah was baking a cherry pie for 8 of her friends. She had a carton of 241 cherries. When she finished the pie, Hannah had 17 cherries left. How many cherries did she use in the pie?

_____

$$200 \times 41$$

$$400 \times 12$$

Day #2

Write each fraction in its simplest form.

$\frac{2}{4}$ = _____

$\frac{3}{9}$ = _____

$\frac{5}{15}$ = _____

Multiples are numbers made by multiplying a number by another number. For example, multiples of 5 are 5, 10, 15, 20…
List 3 multiples for each number.

3 ____, ____, ____

7 ____, ____, ____

9 ____, ____, ____

This clock shows about

○ 5:55   ○ 11:35

○ 11:20   ○ 11:27

```
0000000000000
0000000000000
000000000000
000000000000
00000000000
00000000000
```

How many 0's will be in the sixth box?

_____ 0's

Day #3

Use > or < to compare.

$\frac{1}{8}$ ☐ $\frac{1}{3}$

$\frac{1}{2}$ ☐ $\frac{1}{10}$

$\frac{1}{4}$ ☐ $\frac{1}{12}$

Which is the best estimate for the length of a

paper clip _____
dining table _____
pencil _____
railroad route _____
scissors _____

A. centimeter
B. decimeter
C. meter
D. kilometer

Write each number word.

$\frac{2}{8}$ _____

$\frac{5}{7}$ _____

$\frac{1}{2}$ _____

```
XX
XXX
XXX          5)17
XXX
XXX
XXX
```

```
****** **
*****     3)17
*****
```

Day #4

	January				
1	2	3	4	5	6
7	8	9	10	11	12	13
14	15	16	17	18	19	20
21	22	23	24	25	26	27
28	29	30	31		

Which weeks have the greatest number of odd numbers? _____
Which weeks have the greatest number of even numbers? _____

Eve's number is greater than 15. Dan's number is not evenly divisible by 2. Meg's number is more than Eve's. Ken's number is a prime number.

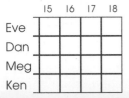

Six hundred twenty-one people bought tickets to the community theater's production of Pinocchio. The tickets cost $4.00 each. Which is the best estimate of the total ticket sales?

○ $1,400

○ $2,400

○ $3,400

If these shapes are placed in a box and one is drawn out, which box, A or B, would give the best chance of drawing a ○? _____

Assessment

1

$$
\begin{array}{r}
100 \\
\times\ 43 \\
\hline
\end{array}
\qquad
\begin{array}{r}
300 \\
\times\ 15 \\
\hline
\end{array}
$$

2

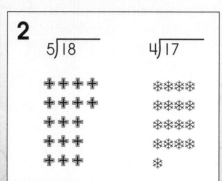

$5\overline{)18}$ $4\overline{)17}$

3 Four hundred seventy-nine people attended the Brigham School's Winter Festival. Each person paid $8.00 for a ticket. About how much did the school make from ticket sales?

○ $4,000   ○ $6,000

○ $5,000   ○ $7,000

4 At a sleepover, Karen and 12 of her friends toasted marshmallows in the fireplace. There were 161 marshmallows in 2 bags. When the girls finished, there were 39 marshmallows leftover. How many marshmallows did they toast? _____

5 Multiples are numbers made by multiplying a number by another number. For example, multiples of 5 are 5, 10, 15, 20... Write the multiples.

8 _____, _____, _____

2 _____, _____, _____

6 Use > or < to compare.

$\dfrac{1}{10}$ ☐ $\dfrac{1}{8}$ $\dfrac{1}{5}$ ☐ $\dfrac{1}{12}$

$\dfrac{1}{4}$ ☐ $\dfrac{1}{2}$ $\dfrac{1}{16}$ ☐ $\dfrac{1}{2}$

7 Which number shows 3 thousands, 9 hundreds, 17 tens, and 2 ones?

○ 4,072

○ 3,979

○ 4,172

○ 5,721

8 Which letter is inside the square and rectangle but not inside the circle?

_____

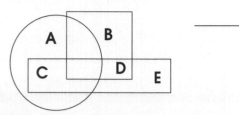

9 This clock shows

○ 2:00

○ 2:30

○ 2:45

○ 2:53

10

February						
	1	2	3	4	5	6
7	8	9	10	11	12	13
14	15	16	17	18	19	20
21	22	23	24	25	26	27
28						

Which week(s) has the greatest number of even numbers? _____

_____

Which week(s) has the greatest number of odd numbers? _____

_____

Day #1

Which number shows 17 hundreds, 3 tens, and 9 ones?

○ 170,039

○ 1,739

○ 10,739

Which letter is inside the square and triangle, but not inside the rectangle or circle? _____

Mickey bought 3 packages of blank cassette tapes to record 17 of his favorite CDs. Each package contained 8 tapes. How many tapes did Mickey buy?

_____

---

900   600
x 55   x 44

Day #2

Reduce.

$\frac{5}{10}$ = _____

$\frac{6}{9}$ = _____

$\frac{12}{16}$ = _____

List 6 multiples for

3 _____, _____, _____

_____, _____, _____

4 _____, _____, _____

_____, _____, _____

6 _____, _____, _____

_____, _____, _____

_____ is the Least Common Multiple for 3, 4, and 6.

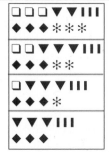

This clock shows

○ 12:07

○ 12:55

○ 1:00

○ 2:10

Draw the 7th box.

Day #3

Use > or < to compare.

$\frac{1}{2}$ ☐ $\frac{1}{20}$

$\frac{1}{42}$ ☐ $\frac{1}{5}$

$\frac{1}{7}$ ☐ $\frac{1}{50}$

Which is the best estimate for the length of a

fever thermometer ____

interstate highway _____

fingernail _____

river _____

tree trunk _____

　　A. centimeter
　　B. decimeter
　　C. meter
　　D. kilometer

Write each number word.

$5\frac{3}{9}$ _____

_____

$6\frac{7}{10}$ _____

_____

$9\frac{1}{5}$ _____

_____

8⟌29

7⟌18

Day #4

S	M	T	W	Th	F	S

Fill in the dates. The third Tuesday is the 13th. Mark the 22nd and the 7th.

On what day of the week does this month begin? _____

Joe's number is greater than 25. Lil's number is a multiple of 5. Hal's number is less than Joe's. Ray's number is divisible by 8.

	20	23	35	40
Joe				
Lil				
Hal				
Ray				

Seventy-eight dollars was spent to buy new trees for the city park. Twelve people paid for the trees. About how much did each person spend?

○ 2 dollars

○ 6 dollars

○ 12 dollars

If these bunnies are in a magician's hat and one is drawn out, it will most likely be a _____ bunny.

Assessment

1

$$200 \times 61$$ $$400 \times 22$$

2

$9\overline{)23}$ $6\overline{)22}$

3

▲▲▲▲
▲▮▰○

If these shapes were in a sack and you drew one out without looking, circle the shape you would most likely draw.

▲ ▮ ▰ ○

4 Write each number word.

$7\frac{5}{8}$ _____

$10\frac{2}{6}$ _____

5 Maria was making a quilt for her 4 cousins. She used 9 material squares for each row. So far, she has sewn 6 rows. How many squares has she used? _____

6 Fill in these calendar dates.

The 15th is on the third Monday. Label the 4th and the 27th. On what day of the week does this month begin? _____

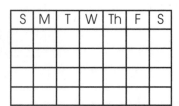

S	M	T	W	Th	F	S

7 This clock shows about

○ 6:00
○ 5:30
○ 6:33
○ 7:30

8 Which is the best estimate for the length of

a ladies handbag _____

the Hoover Dam _____

a toothpick _____

a sidewalk to the front door _____

A. centimeters   B. decimeters

C. meters   D. kilometers

9 Which number has 19 hundreds and 8 tens?

○ 1,908
○ 1,980
○ 190,008
○ 190,080

10 Ninety-one children in a youth group divided into 14 teams to go on a scavenger hunt. What is the best estimate of the number of children on each team?

○ 6
○ 16
○ 60
○ 160

Name

Day #1

Which number shows 3 thousands, 2 hundreds, 15 tens, and 0 ones?

- ○ 30,215
- ○ 3,350
- ○ 3,215

Which figures are polygons?

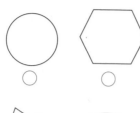

○   ○

○   ○

Ms. Lucas ordered 4 dozen glazed donuts and 10 chocolate donuts. Which method could be used to find the total number of donuts she ordered?

- ○ add 4 and 10
- ○ multiply 4 x 12 and add 10
- ○ subtract 4 from 10 and add 12
- ○ divide 12 by 4 and subtract 10

$$700 \times 35 \qquad 900 \times 42$$

Day #2

$$\frac{2}{6} + \frac{3}{6} = \underline{\quad}$$

$$\frac{4}{10} + \frac{3}{10} = \underline{\quad}$$

A. add   B. multiply

C. divide   D. subtract

_____ to find the quotient

_____ to find the sum

_____ to find the product

_____ to find the difference

Craig bought 9 folders for $0.67 each. How much money did Craig spend on folders?

_____

| ff |
| ffff |
| ffffff |
| ffffffff |

How many fs will be in the ninth box? _____

Day #3

$$\frac{1}{8} \quad \frac{1}{2} \quad \frac{1}{4} \quad \frac{1}{5} \quad \frac{1}{3}$$

Write the fractions above in order from greatest to least. _____

_____

_____

_____

_____

A. grams
B. meters
C. liters
D. centimeters
E. milliliters
F. kilograms
G. kilometers

Mass _____ _____

Distance _____

_____ _____

Volume _____ _____

Which number line shows the whole numbers that are greater than 43 and less than 49? _____

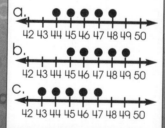

a.
42 43 44 45 46 47 48 49 50

b.
42 43 44 45 46 47 48 49 50

c.
42 43 44 45 46 47 48 49 50

★★★★★★★★
★★★★★★★★
★★★★
★★
★★ ★
★★ ★
★★ ★
★★ ★
★★ ★
★★ ★

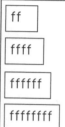

$8\overline{)20}$

$9\overline{)25}$

Day #4

Refreshments Sold at the Festival

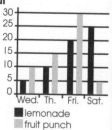

■ lemonade
▨ fruit punch

On which day was more lemonade than fruit punch sold? _____

Joey lives 10 blocks to the east of Ned. Ned lives 2 blocks to the east of Sue. Fran lives 7 blocks to the east of Sue. How many blocks is it from Fran's to Joey's house? _____

How many blocks is it from Fran's to Ned's house? _____

Twenty-one thousand, eight hundred ninety-nine people attended a football game. It began raining and 2,688 people left. About how many people remained at the game?

- ○ 10,000
- ○ 19,000
- ○ 20,000
- ○ 23,000

A ■■□□□□

B ■■□□□□□□

If these tiles are placed in a box and one is drawn out, which box, A or B, would give the best chance of drawing a black tile? _____

Name

Assessment

1

$$\begin{array}{r} 400 \\ \times\ 83 \\ \hline \end{array} \qquad \begin{array}{r} 200 \\ \times\ 79 \\ \hline \end{array}$$

2

$5\overline{)34}\qquad 7\overline{)53}$

3 Thirty-three thousand, five hundred eighty-nine people booked flights in December. Five thousand, one hundred two people canceled their flights because of snowstorms. About how many people kept their flights?

○ 28,000   ○ 30,000

○ 38,000   ○ 20,000

4 For a bake sale, Ms. Murphy baked 7 dozen cookies and 5 cakes. Which method could be used to find the number of baked goods Ms. Murphy prepared?

○ add 7 and 5

○ divide 12 by 5 and add 7

○ subtract 5 from 84

○ multiply 7 by 12 and add 5

5 Match.

A. multiplication   _____ sum

B. division   _____ difference

C. addition   _____ product

D. subtraction   _____ quotient

6

$$\frac{1}{10}\quad \frac{1}{8}\quad \frac{1}{25}\quad \frac{1}{3}\quad \frac{1}{16}$$

Write these fractions in order from least to greatest.

_____, _____, _____, _____, _____

7 Which number shows 6 thousands, 7 hundreds, 12 tens, and 9 ones?

○ 67,129

○ 6,829

○ 6,709

○ 76,129

8 Which figures are polygons?

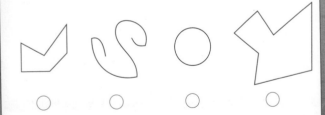

○   ○   ○   ○

9 Lynn sold 8 games at her garage sale. She charged $0.95 for each game. How much money did she make by selling her games at the garage sale?_____

10 The graph shows the points made by the boy's team and the girls' team in a volleyball tournament. In which game did the boys and the girls score the same number of points? _____

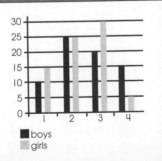

Day #1

Which number shows 22 thousands, 13 hundreds, and 9 ones?

○ 22,139

○ 22,309

○ 23,309

How many faces does this figure have? _____

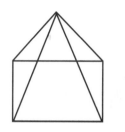

Jamie had 25 sand art packages. She gave 10 to her little sister. Then she bought 8 more. Which equation could be used to find the number of sand art packages Jamie has now?

○ (25 + 10) + 8

○ (25 + 10) – 8

○ (25 – 10) + 8

$$852 \\ \times \quad 5$$

$$437 \\ \times \quad 6$$

Day #2

Subtract.

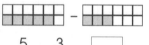

$$\frac{5}{12} - \frac{3}{12} = \boxed{}$$

$$\frac{4}{5} - \frac{2}{5} = \boxed{}$$

Underline the true equations.

(4 x 5) + 3 = 4 x (5 + 3)

(5 x 2) x 2 = 5 x (2 x 2)

(9 x 1) – 1 = 9 x (1 – 1)

(4 x 4) ÷ 1 = 4 x (4 ÷ 1)

Carlos practices his clarinet for one half-hour each day. What is the total number of hours Carlos practices in five days? _____

How many Vs will be in the 20th box? _____

vvvvv

vvvvv
vvvvv

vvvvv
vvvvv
vvvvv

vvvvv
vvvvv
vvvvv
vvvvv

Day #3

$$\frac{2}{15} \quad \frac{2}{12} \quad \frac{2}{9} \quad \frac{2}{42} \quad \frac{2}{5}$$

Write the above fractions in order from greatest to least. _____

_____

_____

_____

Circle the best unit for measuring

1. the distance across Africa

centimeters   decimeters

meters   kilometers

2. the height of a swing set

centimeters   decimeters

meters   kilometers

Write each number using numerals.

four-fifths_____

two-thirds _____

seven-eights _____

Solve.

$$7\overline{)54}$$

$$6\overline{)23}$$

Day #4

Pounds of Recyclables Collected

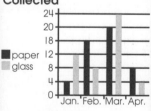

■ paper
■ glass

Comparing totals, the pounds of paper recycled is (>, <, =) to the pounds of recycled glass.

These are klinkers.

These are NOT klinkers.

Which of these are klinkers?

There are 1,460 paintings and 3,977 drawings entered in a children's art festival. There were also 315 collages and 89 clay sculptures entered. About how many total entries were there?

○ between 5,000 and 6,000

○ between 6,000 and 7,000

○ between 4,000 and 5,000

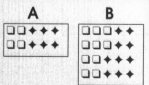

A   B

The chances of drawing a ▢ are

○ greater with box A

○ greater with box B

○ equal with box A or B

Assessment

1

$$\begin{array}{r} 436 \\ \times \ \ 4 \\ \hline \end{array}$$
$$\begin{array}{r} 925 \\ \times \ \ 9 \\ \hline \end{array}$$

2

$8\overline{)77}$ $6\overline{)53}$

3 A | wwwaaaaa |

B | wwwaaa |

The chances of drawing a w from box A are (greater, less, or equal) with drawing a w from box B.

4 Write each fraction using numerals.

seven-ninths_____

four-fifths_____

one-third_____

5 Michael had 72 baseball cards. He traded 20 to his friend for a yo-yo. The next week, Michael got 13 more baseball cards for his birthday. Which equation could be used to find out how many baseball cards Michael has now?

○ (72 − 20) + 13   ○ (72 + 20) + 13

○ 72 − (20 − 13)   ○ 72 + 13

6 A. The total number of votes for football was (>, <, =) the votes for soccer.

B. Which grades had the same number of votes for soccer? grades ____ and ____

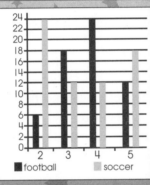

■ football   soccer

7 It takes Maria 15 minutes to walk home from school each day. In 2 weeks, how many hours does she spend walking home from school?

_____

8 Circle the best unit for measuring

A. the height of a house

centimeters   decimeters

meters   kilometers

B. the distance of a trolley ride around town

centimeters   decimeters

meters   kilometers

9 Which number shows 34 thousands, 17 hundreds, and 6 tens?

○ 34,176

○ 35,760

○ 37,460

○ 34,706

10 In a statewide science fair, there were 2,398 projects exhibited on recycling and 1,598 projects on solar energy. The fair also had 79 ecology projects and 221 electricity projects. About how many projects were exhibited at the science fair?

○ between 2,000 and 3,000

○ between 3,000 and 4,000

○ between 4,000 and 5,000

○ between 5,000 and 6,000

Which number shows 10 thousands, 22 hundreds, and 4 tens?

○ 12,240

○ 20,224

○ 22,104

How many faces does this figure have? _____

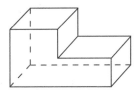

Xavier shared a package of 37 pizza bites with 4 of his friends. If all the boys ate the same number of pizza bites, how many were left over?

_____

705
x   6

$\frac{5}{9} + \frac{2}{9} =$ _____

$\frac{3}{12} + \frac{7}{12} =$ _____

Day #1

Write each fraction as a whole number or mixed number in its simplest form.

$\frac{24}{3}$ _____

$\frac{30}{7}$ _____

Underline the true equations.

$(9 + 8) + 7 = 9 + (8 + 7)$

$(8 \times 4) \times 0 = 8 \times (4 \times 0)$

$(12 - 3) - 2 = 12 - (3 - 2)$

$(6 \times 6) \div 1 = 6 \times (6 \div 1)$

**Computer Lab
Minutes of Time Used
per Week**

Grade	M	T	W	Th	F
3	15		15		
4		30		45	
5	15		60		15

For the week shown, how many minutes was the computer lab used?

_____ minutes =

_____ hours _____ minutes

384

192

96

48

What number will be in the 7th box?

☐

Day #2

$\frac{30}{3}$ $\frac{4}{2}$ $\frac{16}{2}$ $\frac{20}{5}$

Write the fractions in order from least to greatest.

_____

_____

_____

_____

What is the area of the figure shown on the grid?

_____ square units

Write each mixed number using numerals.

six and seven-tenths

_____

ten and four-fifths

_____

fifteen and eight-twentieths

_____

$4\overline{)84}$

$\frac{7}{16} - \frac{4}{16} =$ _____

$\frac{4}{5} - \frac{3}{5} =$ _____

Day #3

Temperatures for the School Week

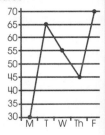

The greatest difference in temperature occurred between which two days? _____ and _____

These are gloopies.

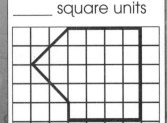

These are NOT gloopies.

Which of these are gloopies?

Two thousand, three hundred seventy-eight people came on the opening day of the county fair. One thousand, nine hundred thirty-two people came the next day. On the third day, 781 people came, and on the last day, 1,032 people came. About how many people came to the fair?

○ between 4,000 and 5,000

○ between 5,000 and 6,000

○ between 6,000 and 7,000

The chances of drawing a ▲ are

○ greater than drawing a ✛

○ less than drawing a ✛

○ equal to drawing a ✛

Day #4

Assessment

1

$$903 \times 7 \qquad 201 \times 8$$

2

$$4\overline{)88} \qquad 2\overline{)64}$$

3 Seven thousand, eight hundred two visitors attended the museum's African exhibit. Two thousand, one hundred seven visitors attended the Egyptian exhibit, and 5,890 visitors saw the Japanese exhibit. About how many visitors attended these exhibits?

○ between 14,000 and 15,000
○ between 15,000 and 16,000
○ between 16,000 and 17,000

4 Natasha bought a package of cookies to share with her 6 friends. The package contained 45 cookies. If Natasha and her friends each get the same number of cookies, how many cookies will be leftover? _____

5 Which equations are true?

○ $(12 + 5) - 4 = 12 + (5 - 4)$
○ $(6 \times 5) \times 0 = 6 \times (5 \times 0)$
○ $(9 \times 8) \div 1 = 9 \times (8 \div 1)$
○ $(14 - 5) - 2 = 14 - (5 - 2)$

6 $\dfrac{25}{5} \quad \dfrac{21}{7} \quad \dfrac{30}{5} \quad \dfrac{18}{9} \quad \dfrac{54}{6}$

Write the above fractions in order from greatest to least.

____ ____ ____ ____ ____

7 Which number shows 50 thousands, 35 hundreds, and 4 tens?

○ 50,354
○ 55,304
○ 53,540
○ 5,354

8 How many faces does this figure have? _____

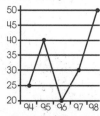

9 Minutes of Science Lab Time Used per Week

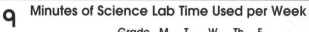

Grade	M	T	W	Th	F
2	30		30		30
3	45			45	
4	20	20	20		30

For the week shown on the chart, how many minutes was the science lab in use?

_____ minutes = _____ hours _____ minutes

10 Average Temperature for February

50
45
40
35
30
25
20
94 95 96 97 98

The graph shows the average temperature for the month of February during the years 1994–1998.

During which two years was the difference in the average temperature the greatest?

_____ and _____   _____ and _____

During which two years was it the least?

_____ and _____

Name

Week # 28

Chama flipped through the dictionary. The page he landed on had a 4 in the ones place, a 5 in the thousands place, and a 2 in the tens place. What was Chama's page number? _____

How many corners does this figure have? _____

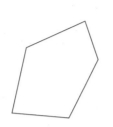

Mrs. Hernandez made coffee for the 7 members of her bridge club. Her coffee maker makes 30 cups. If she and her club members drink an equal number of cups, how many cups of coffee will still be in the coffee maker when her guests leave? _____

22 }
$\times 13$

$20 + 2$
$\times 3$

34
$\times 32$

$20 + 2$
$\times 10$

Write each fraction as a whole number or mixed number in its simplest form.

$\frac{31}{3} =$ _____

$\frac{45}{7} =$ _____

Which equation does NOT belong?

◯ $7 \times 8 = 56$

◯ $8 \times 7 = 56$

◯ $56 \div 8 = 7$

◯ $7 + 8 = 15$

What time will the clock show in 2 hours and 45 minutes? _____

| 9 |
| 18 |
| 27 |
| 36 |

What number will be in the 10th box?

Use >, <, or = to compare.

$\frac{4}{2}$ ☐ $1\frac{1}{5}$

$2\frac{3}{8}$ ☐ $\frac{20}{4}$

$5\frac{2}{8}$ ☐ $\frac{42}{8}$

What is the area of the figure shown on the grid?

_____ square units

What is the approximate perimeter?

_____ units

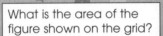
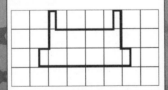

A

$\overline{12 \quad 13 \quad 14 \quad 15 \quad 16}$

Which mixed number belongs where you see the letter A?

◯ $15\frac{1}{32}$

◯ $15\frac{1}{2}$

◯ $15\frac{7}{8}$

$7\overline{)490}$

$9\overline{)1,800}$

Plant Growth After 3 Weeks

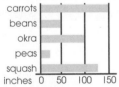

inches 0   50   100   150

Circle the best estimate of the growth difference between the squash and peas.

100 in.   150 in.   50 in.

Use the graph to the left. Together the peas and the _____ grew about the same as the squash.

Shade the chart below that matches the graph.

carrots	150	carrots	150
beans	50	beans	50
okra	100	okra	100
peas	25	peas	50
squash	125	squash	100

Three thousand, five hundred ninety-three people were seated on 9 rows of stadium bleachers. About how many people were sitting on each row?

◯ 200

◯ 300

◯ 400

◯ 500

Tymo wants to mount his 6 miniature puzzles in one frame. What information does Tymo need before buying the frame?

◯ the number of pieces in each puzzle

◯ the combined areas of the puzzles

◯ the cost of the puzzles

Assessment

1

$$\begin{array}{r} 31 \\ \times 12 \\ \hline \end{array}$$
$$\begin{array}{r} 13 \\ \times 23 \\ \hline \end{array}$$

2

$$6\overline{)360}\quad\quad 8\overline{)5,600}$$

3

| 12 |
| 24 |
| 36 |
| 48 |

What number will be in the 8th box? [ ]

4

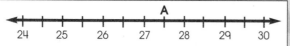

24 25 26 27 28 29 30

Which mixed number belongs where you see the letter A?

○ $26\frac{1}{2}$ ○ $27\frac{1}{8}$ ○ $27\frac{11}{12}$ ○ $27\frac{1}{2}$

5 Jeff's mother made pizzas for his birthday. She sliced the pizzas into 50 slices. She served Jeff and his 7 guests the same number of slices, and she ate the rest. How many pieces of pizza did Jeff's mother eat? _____

6

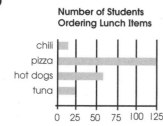

Number of Students Ordering Lunch Items

chili
pizza
hot dogs
tuna

0   25   50   75   100   125

Complete the chart.	
Item	Number Ordered
tuna	____
____	15
____	55
pizza	____

7 What time will the clock show in 4 hours and 15 minutes? _____

8 What is the area of the figure shown on the grid? _____ square units

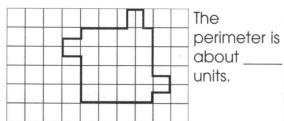

The perimeter is about ____ units.

9 Heather wrote a number with a 6 in the ones place, a 2 in the thousands place, and a 9 in the tens place. What number did Heather write?

_____

10 Five thousand, five hundred twenty-one illustrations are included in a 6 volume set of children's dictionaries. About how many illustrations are in each volume?

○ 600

○ 700

○ 800

○ 900

Day #1

Leslie was writing the populations of several cities. The population of Nawton has a 9 in the thousands place, a 5 in the ones place, and a 6 in the ten thousands place. What number did Leslie write for Nawton's population?

_____

How many corners does this figure have? _____

Adam is studying for an end-of-semester spelling test. There are 6 word lists that have 15 words each. Adam studies for his spelling test by writing the words three times. How many words will Adam write? _____

$$45 \atop \underline{\times 25}$$

$$40 + 5 \atop \underline{\times 5}$$

$$40 + 5 \atop \underline{\times 20}$$

$$62 \atop \underline{\times 43}$$

Day #2

Add or subtract. Simplify if needed.

$\frac{5}{8} + \frac{2}{8} =$ _____

$\frac{2}{10} + \frac{1}{10} =$ _____

$\frac{4}{6} - \frac{2}{6} =$ _____

To find the average of a group of numbers, add the numbers together. Then divide the total by the number of addends.

Find the average for

8, 7, 2, 3, 15

_____

Robert saved $52.00 so he could attend a concert. He paid $23.50 for the tickets. At the concert, he bought a program for $7.25 and a T-shirt for $15.00. How much money did Robert have after the concert? _____

88, 81, 74, 67, 60

What is the rule for the pattern?

_____

_____

Day #3

Use >, <, or = to compare.

$\frac{9}{3}$ ☐ $3\frac{1}{3}$

$7\frac{1}{4}$ ☐ $\frac{30}{4}$

$2\frac{1}{16}$ ☐ $\frac{20}{4}$

Use >, <, or = to compare.

3 inches	☐	3 yards
6 feet	☐	2 yards
12 inches	☐	1 foot
8 feet	☐	1 yard

Which mixed number belongs where you see the letter A?

○ $13\frac{1}{2}$

○ $12\frac{1}{2}$

○ $12\frac{3}{4}$

$3\overline{)9,360}$

$4\overline{)8,048}$

Day #4

James ☘☘☘☘☘

Kevin ☘☘☘☘☘

Steve ☘☘☘☘☘

each ☘ = 8

Shade in the graph to show that Kevin trimmed 36 trees. Steve trimmed 44 trees. James trimmed 20 trees.

Use the graph to the left. How many trees were trimmed by all the boys? _____

One-half a tree shaded = _____ trees

Steve trimmed about _____ times the number of trees trimmed by James.

One thousand, five hundred ninety-three people were waiting to board 8 planes. About how many passengers will get on each plane?

○ 100

○ 200

○ 300

○ 400

Mrs. Jordan needs to make lemonade for the school's field day. A can of lemonade serves 30 people. What information does Mrs. Jordan need before she makes the lemonade?

○ the cost of the lemonade per can

○ how many cans it takes to make a gallon

○ the number of people who will drink lemonade

Assessment

1

$$\begin{array}{r} 67 \\ \times\ 26 \\ \hline \end{array} \qquad \begin{array}{r} 39 \\ \times\ 47 \\ \hline \end{array}$$

2

$7\overline{)4,200}$ $\qquad$ $8\overline{)5,600}$

3 During 1 week, 5,598 people booked tours. The tour line has 7 buses. About how many people did each bus carry during the week?

○ 600
○ 700
○ 800
○ 900

4 During 25 days at summer camp, Lisbet swam 3 times a day. She swam 20 meters each time. How many meters did Lisbet swim during summer camp? _____

5 Find the average for this group of numbers.

17, 3, 12, 8, 5 _____

6 Use >, <, or = to compare.

4 ☐ $\dfrac{12}{3}$

$2\dfrac{4}{5}$ ☐ $2\dfrac{6}{5}$

$5\dfrac{7}{3}$ ☐ $7\dfrac{1}{3}$

7 Weston used his computer's word count on a report he was writing. The computer counted the words in his report and displayed a 9 in the hundreds place. How many words were in Weston's report? _____

8 How many corners does the figure have? _____

9 Javier saved $72.30 to buy some new computer games. He bought Rocket Race for $22.77 and Pro Ball for $19.85. The tax on the two CDs was $5.75. How much did Javier have after buying the games? _____

10 Add or subtract. Write the answer in simplest form.

$\dfrac{3}{7} + \dfrac{1}{7} =$ ____ $\qquad$ $\dfrac{6}{16} - \dfrac{2}{16} =$ ____ $\qquad$ $\dfrac{7}{9} - \dfrac{5}{9} =$ ____

Day #1

30,000 + 7,000 + 200 + 3 =

- ○ 37,230
- ○ 372,003
- ○ 30,702,003
- ○ 37,203

Write C if the figures are congruent. Write S if they are similar.

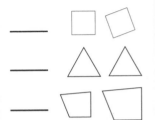

____

____

____

Neva bought 3 packages of gum. Each package has 12 pieces. How can Neva share the gum with 8 of her friends so that she and her friends each get the same number of pieces?

_____

```
   15
 x 75
```

```
 6,247
+4,788
```

Day #2

Add or subtract. Simplify.

$\frac{5}{12} + \frac{4}{12} =$ ____

$\frac{8}{13} - \frac{5}{13} =$ ____

$\frac{12}{32} + \frac{12}{32} =$ ____

The range of a group of numbers is the difference between the least and the greatest number in the group. The median of a group of numbers is the middle number when the group is arranged from least to greatest.

8, 5, 3, 20, 2

range = ____

median = ____

Janette bought nail polish for $3.89, 2 tubes of lip gloss for $2.49 each, and perfume for $9.22. The total after tax was added was $19.54. How much tax did Janette pay on the items she bought?

_____

2, 9, 23, 51, 107

What is the rule for the pattern?

_____

_____

Day #3

Some of the Largest Earth-Filled Dams Measured in Cubic Yards

Tarbela	186,000,000
Oahe	92,000,000
Cornelia	274,026,000
Pati	261,590
Atatürk	110,522

List the names of the dams in order of size from least to greatest. _____

_____   _____

_____   _____

Use >, <, or = to compare.

24 inches ☐ 3 feet

9 feet ☐ 3 yards

36 inches ☐ 1 yard

10 feet ☐ 2 yards

Which number is read two hundred seventy-five million, nine hundred thousand, forty-six?

- ○ 275,900,046
- ○ 275,946
- ○ 200,759,460

5)4,525

9)7,245

Day #4

Margie's Gift Wrapping

Sept.	■ ■ ■ ■ ▪
Oct.	■ ■ ▪
Nov.	■ ■ ■ ■ ■ ■ ▪
Dec.	■ ■ ■ ■ ■ ■ ■ ▪

each ■ = 50 gifts wrapped

How many gifts were wrapped in October?_____

How many gifts were wrapped in September? _____

Use the graph to the left. How many gifts were wrapped during all four months? _____

How many more gifts were wrapped in November and December than were wrapped in September?_____

How many more ■ would be needed to show 250 gifts wrapped in October? _____

What is 675,789 rounded to the nearest thousand?

- ○ 700,000
- ○ 676,000
- ○ 680,000
- ○ 674,000

Shane spent $25.00 on vacation souvenirs. His mother spent $40.00, and his dad spent $30.00. Judy, Shane's sister, spent more than Shane and Dad but less than Mother. Which could be true?

- ○ Judy spent $45.00.
- ○ Judy spent $32.00.
- ○ Judy spent $29.00.

Assessment

1

$$69$$
$$\times 47$$

$$3,987$$
$$+4,776$$

2

$$4\overline{)3,624}$$ $$3\overline{)1,512}$$

3   6, 21, 66, 201

What is the rule for the above pattern?

_____

_____

4   Match.

1. three hundred ninety-five million, two hundred six thousand, four hundred one _____

2. three million, ninety-five thousand, two hundred sixty-one _____

3. thirty-nine thousand, two hundred sixty-four _____

A. 395,206,401   B. 39,264   C. 3,095,261

5   Ron bought 3 boxes of juice drinks for his track team. Each box contains 6 drinks. If Ron and his 8 team members each have the same number of juice drinks, how many will each person receive? _____

6   **Operator Assisted Phone Calls from Hotel Farrington**

May   ☎ ☎ ☎ ☎

June   ☎ ☎ ☎ ☎ ☎   each ☎ = 80

July   ☎ ☎ ☎ ☎ ☎ ☎ ☎ ☎

Aug.   ☎ ☎ ☎ ☎ ☎ ☎

How many calls were made in June? _____
How many calls were made in August? _____
How many more calls were made in August than in May? _____
In all, how many calls were made? _____

7   Emil earned $57.00 doing odd jobs. Mark earned more than Emil, but less than Jake. Jake earned $72.00. Which could be true?

○ Mark earned $55.00.

○ Mark earned $75.00.

○ Mark earned $67.00.

8   Use >, < or = to compare.

36 inches	☐	2 feet
3 yards	☐	9 feet
24 inches	☐	1 foot
1 yard	☐	24 inches

9

$60,000 + 3,000 + 500 + 4 =$ _____

$500,000 + 80,000 + 2,000 + 1 =$ _____

$20,000 + 300 + 90 + 7 =$ _____

10   What is 782,432 rounded to the nearest thousand?

○ 780,000

○ 790,000

○ 781,400

○ 782,000

What is 816,120 rounded to the nearest thousand?

○ 810,000

○ 816,000

○ 822,400

○ 825,000

Day # 1

500,000 + 30,000 + 400 + 20 + 7 =

- ○ 530,427
- ○ 500,003,427
- ○ 53,427
- ○ 534,270

Write C if the figures are congruent. Write S if they are similar.

Mrs. Baker picked 22 red flowers, 40 yellow flowers, 58 miniature daisies, and 24 white flower buds from her garden. She places the same number of plants in each of 4 baskets. How many plants are in each basket? _____

```
  315
x   7
```

```
  7,938
+ 2,677
```

Day # 2

Add or subtract the fractions. Simplify.

$9\frac{5}{7} - 4\frac{4}{7} =$ _____

$3\frac{1}{12} + 7\frac{5}{12} =$ _____

$16\frac{8}{24} - 5\frac{5}{24} =$ _____

Find the median, range, and mean for the following group of numbers.

13, 57, 23, 42, 15

median = _____

range = _____

mean = _____

What time will the clock show in 2 hours and 25 minutes? _____

| 1, 1 | 2, 4 | 3, 9 |

| 4, 16 | 5, 25 |

What would the 8th box look like?

Day # 3

Some Famous Volcanoes— Height in Feet

Aconcagua	22,831
Lassen	10,457
Mauna Loa	13,677
Cotopaxi	19,347
Mt. Etna	11,122

List the names of the volcanoes in order of height from greatest to least.

_____, _____,

_____, _____,

_____

The temperature on this thermometer shows about ____ degrees Celsius.

Which number is read three million, nine hundred sixty-two thousand, four hundred twenty-one

- ○ 396,241
- ○ 3,962,421
- ○ 300,962,421

```
  8,247
- 5,872
```

```
  5,104
- 2,652
```

Day # 4

Average Temperature

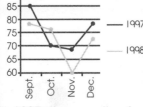

In 1997, the month of _____ had about the same temperature as the month of _____ in 1998.

| 2 | 12 | 5 | 7 |
| 9 | 11 | 3 | 6 |

If 3 bean bags were tossed onto the above board so that no number was repeated, what could be a possible score?

- ○ 50   ○ 8
- ○ 32   ○ 100

Round these numbers to the nearest ten thousand.

775,320 _____

621,990 _____

482,589 _____

907,125 _____

Using only the above beads, what is a possible arrangement?

- ○
- ○
- ○

Assessment

1

$$209 \quad\quad 8,356$$
$$\underline{\times\ \ 8} \quad \underline{+ 3,784}$$

2

$$6,159$$
$$\underline{- 4,882}$$

---

3 Round these numbers to the nearest ten thousand.

884,298 _____

466,132 _____

525,017 _____

---

4 Andy bought 55 gumdrops, 82 peppermints, 50 sour balls, and 35 lemon drops to fill 6 candy jars for the nursing home. How many pieces of candy will he put in each jar?

_____

---

5 Find the median, range, and mean for this group of numbers.

13, 12, 5, 26, 11, 8, 9

median _____

range _____

mean _____

---

6 List the months in order from greatest to least amount of water used for lawn care.

_____

_____

_____

_____

Gallons of Water Used for Lawn Care in Reskin, Illinois	
May	89,129
June	92,456
July	89,752
August	92,488

---

7 900,000 + 80,000 + 2,000 + 400 + 80 =

_____

70,000 + 1,000 + 50 + 1 =

_____

200,000 + 3,000 + 600 + 70 + 8 =

_____

---

8 Write C if the figures are congruent. Write S if they are similar.

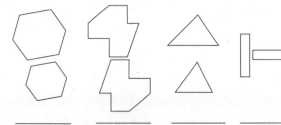 

_____   _____

---

9 What time will the clock show in 2 hours and 35 minutes? _____

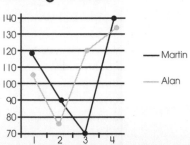

---

10 **Bowling Scores**

During which game did Alan and Martin score about the same? _____

During which game was the difference in their scores the greatest? _____

Day #1

Write in expanded form.

43,209

_____

_____

_____

_____

Label S for slide and F for flip.

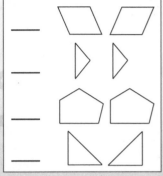

____

____

____

____

Angie had 408 stickers on 8 pages of her sticker album. If each page has the same number of stickers, which equation could be used to show the number of stickers on each page?

○ 408 + 8 = 416

○ 408 – 8 = 400

○ 408 x 8 = 3,264

○ 408 ÷ 8 = 51

$$942 \times 8$$

$$9,527 + 4,658$$

Day #2

Simplify.

$3\frac{16}{12}$ = ____

$9\frac{24}{8}$ = ____

$7\frac{32}{6}$ = ____

Find the median, range, and mean for this group of numbers.

2, 16, 32, 15, 3, 9, 7

median = _____

range = _____

mean = _____

Tristan arrives at school at 8:15. He has 4 hours and 20 minutes of classes until lunch time. At what time does Tristan eat lunch?

_____

| 1, 4 | 2, 5 | 3, 6 |

| 4, 7 | 5, 8 |

What would the 21st box look like?

[ ]

Day #3

Which group of numbers is in order from greatest to least?

○ 7,234; 7,432; 7,243

○ 8,021; 8,012; 8,003

○ 5,921; 5,812; 5,993

○ 2,005; 2,415; 2,501

Shade in this thermometer to show about 75 degrees Celsius.

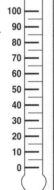

This number line shows

300 305 310 315 320

○ multiples of 5 between 305 and 345

○ multiples of 10 between 300 and 330

○ multiples of 5 between 295 and 325

$$5,040 - 3,217$$

$$9,200 - 7,643$$

Day #4

Money Earned Doing Odd Jobs

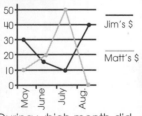

Jim's $

Matt's $

During which month did Jim and Matt earn about the same amount of money? _____

If 3 darts burst three of the above balloons, what could be a possible score?

○ 50

○ 45

○ 15

○ 38

A reasonable estimate of the number of hours a fourth-grade student might spend doing homework during the week would be about

○ 100 hours

○ 45 hours

○ 5 hours

○ 1 hour

Might Marvels Video Game

Player	Score
Jason	2,450
Roger	3,100
Alex	4,200

The answer is 1,750. Using the chart, write a question for this answer.

Assessment

1

$$934 \times 7$$ $$6,107 + 7,999$$

2

$$8,020 - 2,731$$

3

| 10, 9 | 20, 19 |
| 30, 29 | 40, 39 |

What would the 12th box look like? ☐

4

196 200 204 208 212 216 220 224 228

This number line shows

○ multiples of 2 between 194 and 230

○ multiples of 4 between 192 and 232

○ multiples of 5 between 195 and 230

5 Kyle has 105 models on 5 shelves. If each shelf has the same number of models, which equation could be used to find the number of models on each shelf?

○ $105 \div 5 = 21$ ○ $105 \times 5 = 525$

○ $105 - 5 = 100$ ○ $105 + 5 = 110$

6

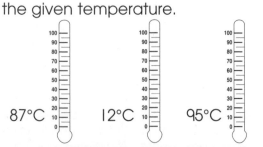

Pages Read by Kay and Gina

60 50 40 30 20 10 0

Mon. Tues. Wed. Thurs.

—— Kay —— Gina

On which day was the difference in pages read the greatest?_____
On which day was the difference in pages read the least? _____
On which day did both girls read more than 35 pages? _____

7 Summer school classes begin at 8:45 AM and last for 4 and a half hours. At what time do summer school classes end? _____

8 Shade in each thermometer to show the given temperature.

87°C 12°C 95°C

(thermometers marked 0 to 100)

9 Write the expanded form.

27,170 _____

_____

50,936 _____

_____

10 A reasonable estimate of the number of hours a student might spend watching television during the school week would be about

○ 1 hour

○ 10 hours

○ 100 hours

○ 1,000 hours

Day #1

Write in expanded form.

390,682

_____

_____

_____

_____

Label S for slide and F for flip.

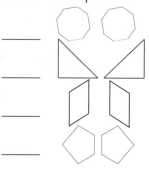

____

____

____

Luis is reading a novel for a book report due on Friday. His novel has 150 pages. He read 27 pages on Monday, 42 pages on Tuesday, and 59 pages on Wednesday. How many more pages must he read to finish the book? _____

$$\begin{array}{r} 42 \\ \times\ 20 \\ \hline \end{array}$$

$$\begin{array}{r} 93 \\ \times\ 30 \\ \hline \end{array}$$

Day #2

Add and simplify.

$2\frac{1}{3} + 8\frac{2}{3} =$ _____

$4\frac{3}{12} + 7\frac{10}{12} =$ _____

$9\frac{1}{4} + 5\frac{3}{4} =$ _____

Bowling League Finals

Team	Points Scored
A	767
B	906
C	760
D	851
E	593

Which teams scored an odd number of points? _____

Sheila saw these ads in the newspaper.

Maxi's Essentials	Sav-Co
$19.95	$21.98
$2.98	$15.25
☎ $25.00	☎ $2.50

How much money can Sheila save by buying the three items at Sav-Co? _____

		35	42
49	56	63	

What numbers go in the three empty boxes? _____

_____

_____

Day #3

Which group of numbers is in order from least to greatest?

○ 6,434; 6,532; 6,943

○ 5,021; 5,012; 5,003

○ 9,921; 8,812; 8,983

○ 1,005; 1,015; 1,001

The keys weigh

grams

○ 1 gram

○ more than 1 gram

○ less than 1 gram

○ 100 grams

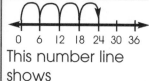

0 6 12 18 24 30 36

This number line shows

○ 24 − 6 = 19

○ 24 ÷ 2 = 12

○ 6 × 4 = 24

○ 6 + 6 + 6 + 6 = 24

$$\begin{array}{r} 9{,}010 \\ -\ 8{,}736 \\ \hline \end{array}$$

$6\overline{)636}$

Day #4

Bicycle Color Choices

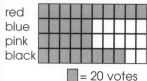

red
blue
pink
black

☐ = 20 votes

Circle the true statements.
A. The number of people who chose red was twice the number who chose blue.
B. Blue received the fewest votes.

Use the graph to the left.
C. Pink received 60 votes.
D. Black received 20 less votes than red.
E. Blue received 100 votes.
F. The difference between the number of votes received by black and blue is 60.
G. The number of votes received by pink is one-half those received by black.

If you use one sheet of notebook paper for each of four different subjects every day, about how many sheets of notebook paper will you use in two weeks?

○ 200 sheets

○ 100 sheets

○ 40 sheets

○ 5 sheets

Greg ate 3 slices of pizza. Joey ate 3 times as many as Greg, but 4 less than mark. Mario ate 2 more slices than Greg. On the back of this paper, write a question for each answer given below.

A. 5 slices

B. 13 slices

C. 30 slices

Assessment

I

$$\begin{array}{r} 64 \\ \times\ 20 \\ \hline \end{array} \qquad \begin{array}{r} 4{,}070 \\ -\ 2{,}398 \\ \hline \end{array}$$

2

$$8\overline{)648}$$

3 Billy read an average of 7 pages a night during the school week. About how many pages will he read in 3 weeks?

○ 35   ○ 50
○ 100   ○ 135

4 Jay's baseball team set a goal of getting 5 more runs this season than in the last 3 seasons combined. In 2002, the team had 23 runs, in 2003 the team had 19 runs, and in 2004, they had 14 runs. So far this year, they have 17 runs. How many more runs does Jay's team need in order to meet their goal? _____

5

Number of Babysitting Jobs Last Year		Which girls had an even number of babysitting jobs last year?
Milly	72	
Jean	24	
Susan	63	_____
Andrea	41	
Carla	58	_____

6 Which group of numbers is in order from least to greatest?

○ 7,892; 7,880, 7,782

○ 5,208; 5,590; 5,579

○ 6,890; 6,895; 6,080

○ 3,207; 3,227; 3,303

7 Write the expanded form.

801,267 _____

_____

420,198 _____

_____

8 Label S for slide and F for flip.

___   ___

___   ___

9 Mrs. Amyx usually buys burgers at Dot's Drive-In, but this week Busy B's is having a sale. How much will Mrs. Amyx save by buying 4 burgers, 4 fries, and 4 shakes at Busy B's? _____

Dot's Drive-In		Busy B's	
4 burgers	$14.45	4 burgers	$12.25
4 fries	$8.75	4 fries	$7.50
4 shakes	$8.80	4 shakes	$8.00

10 Add or subtract. Simplify the fractions.

$$15\frac{3}{7} - 7\frac{5}{7} = \_\_\_\_ \qquad 6\frac{9}{18} + 8\frac{11}{18} = \_\_\_\_ \qquad 5\frac{5}{20} + 9\frac{15}{20} = \_\_\_\_$$

Day #1

Which number shows 7 hundred thousands, 12 ten thousands, 4 hundreds, and 2 tens?

○ 701,242

○ 712,042

○ 820,420

○ 802,452

Name the vertex of each angle.

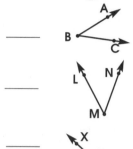

_____

_____

_____

Before dieting, Debra weighed 132 pounds. She lost an average of 2 pounds a month last year. Which equation shows how to find Debra's current weight?

○ 132 – 2 = 130

○ 132 – (2 x 12) = 108

○ 132 ÷ (2 x 6) = 11

$$267 \times 300$$

$$578 \times 600$$

Day #2

Write the fraction and the decimal shown by each model.

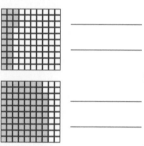

_____

_____

_____

_____

Which number could be a remainder when dividing by 6?

○ 4

○ 7

○ 9

Which number could be a remainder when dividing by 10?

○ 15

○ 25

○ 8

Ms. Wan needs 2 pounds of coffee, 6 pounds of sugar, and 20 paper plates. Which store will save her money on these items? _____

Food Town

1 pound coffee	$3.50
2 pound bag sugar	$2.00
10 pack paper plates	$2.25

Mini Market

2 pounds coffee	$7.50
3 pound bag sugar	$2.50
5 pack paper plates	$1.00

			57
63	69	75	81

What numbers go in the three empty boxes? _____

_____

_____

Day #3

Dictionary	Number of Entry Words
Maridim's	467,897
Collegiate	674,987
Duke Press	460,809
Gorktles	669,989

List the dictionaries in order from the least number of entry words to the greatest number.

_____

_____

_____

_____

grams

The paper fan weighs

○ 3 grams

○ more than 9 grams

○ less than 9 grams

○ 9 grams

Write the number word for

45,206 _____

_____

631,520 _____

$$2,000 - 1,218$$

$$4\overline{)929}$$

Day #4

Garden	Flowers Blooming
Mrs. Willis	24
Ms. Jones	36
Mr. Bates	44
Miss Sax	52

Draw a picture graph on the back of this paper that shows the chart data above.

each ❀ = 8

Mystery Numbers

A = C ÷ 7

B = a multiple of 5 less than 20

C = B + 6

D = A x C

A = _____

B = _____

C = _____

D = _____

Round each number to the nearest 10.

467,125 _____

235,942 _____

551,932 _____

248,701 _____

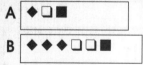

The chances of drawing a ◆ are

○ equal between box A and B

○ greater with box B

○ greater with box A

Assessment

1

$$398 \times 600 \qquad 5{,}000 \times 4{,}231$$

2

$5\overline{)288}$

3

			65
74	83	92	101

What numbers go in the three empty boxes?

_____, _____, _____

4 Write the number words.

503,291 _____

_____

48,603 _____

_____

5 Eight months ago Tad weighed 98 pounds. He has gained an average of 3 pounds a month. Which equation could be used to find Tad's current weight?

○ $98 - 8 = 90$ ○ $98 - (3 \times 8) = 74$

○ $98 \times 3 = 294$ ○ $98 + (3 \times 8) = 122$

6

Snow Cones Sold

Blueberry Ice	33	Coconut Freeze	27
Mocha Cream	18	Cherry Blizzard	42

Shade the graph to match the chart data above.

 = 6

Blueberry Ice
Mocha Cream
Coconut Freeze
Cherry Blizzard

7

Apple School Supply		ABC School Supply	
10 pencils	$5.00	5 pencils	$2.00
notebook	$12.50	2 notebooks	$26.00
writing tablets	3 for $3.75	writing tablets	2 for $3.50

Raul needs to buy 1 pencil, 2 notebooks, and 5 writing tablets for school. Which store will save him the most money on these items? _____

8

grams

The plastic lamp weighs about _____ grams.

9 Which number shows 9 hundred thousands, 25 ten thousands, and 7 tens?

○ 1,150,070

○ 900,250,070

○ 9,257

○ 902,507

10 Round each number to the nearest 100,000.

872,559 _____

430,925 _____

289,601 _____

Day #1

Which number shows 2 million, 17 hundred thousands, 8 ten thousands, 4 tens, and 3 ones?

○ 3,780,043

○ 2,170,843

○ 3,878,403

○ 2,170,800,443

How many vertices are in the figures below?

_____

_____

Luigi sold a total of 1,321 raffle tickets in 3 weeks. He sold 467 tickets the first week and 299 tickets the second week. How many tickets did Luigi sell in the third week?

_____

```
   52
 x 33
```


```
   28
 x 56
```

Day #2

Write the fraction and the decimal shown by each model.

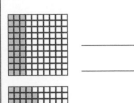
_____
_____

_____
_____

Which number could be a remainder when dividing by 9?

○ 12

○ 7

○ 9

Which number could be a remainder when dividing by 3?

○ 10

○ 5

○ 1

Floyd and Kyle have 17 Super Pounce video games, 13 Blasto Control video games, and 20 Constellation video games. If they played each game for 30 minutes, could they play all the games in one day?_____

_____

○ ○ ✳ ✳ ✳ ✗ ✗
✶ ✓ ✶ ✓ ○ ○ ✳

Which series below would continue the pattern? _____

A. ✳ ✳ ✳ ✗ ✶ ✓

B. ✗ ✗ ✶ ✓ ✶ ✓

C. ✳ ✳ ✗ ✗ ✶ ✓

Day #3

Write the number that is 100 more than

234,967 _____

529,920 _____

862,425 _____

999,901 _____

| 1 cup = 8 ounces |
| 1 pint = 2 cups |
| 1 quart = 2 pints |
| 1 gallon = 4 quarts |

3 gallons = _____ quarts

5 pints = _____ cups

8 quarts = _____ pints

1 quart = _____ ounces

Write the number words.

2,450,137

_____

_____

5,320,664

_____

_____

```
6)727
```


```
4)838
```

Day #4

red = 36   green = 48

blue = 24   black = 12

To correctly color the pie graph so that it matches the above data, each section must stand for the same number. Determine that number, then color in the graph.

each part

= _____

Mystery Numbers

A = 18 – (D x D)

B = C ÷ 4

C = D + A

D = the remainder of 47 ÷ 9

A = _____

B = _____

C = _____

D = _____

On Tuesday, Jet Air sold 45,951 airline tickets. Concourse Flights sold 31,764 tickets, and Miami Intrastate sold 18,752 tickets. What is the best estimate of the number of tickets sold by all 3 airlines?

○ 100,000 tickets

○ 125,000 tickets

○ 150,000 tickets

A ⌈ L L B B B ⌉

B ⌈ L L L L B ⌉

The chances of drawing an L are

○ equal between box A and B

○ less with box B

○ 2 times greater with box B

Assessment

1

98	41
x 52	x 61

2

$9\overline{)748}$

3 CompuCom made 55,210 computer chips in March, 71,560 chips in April, and 66,102 chips in May. What is the best estimate of the number of computer chips made in all three months?

○ 250,000   ○ 150,000

○ 200,000   ○ 100,000

4 Megan's Girl Scout troop collected 1,072 pounds of aluminum cans last summer. In June, they collected 397 pounds and in July they collected 289 pounds. How many pounds of aluminum cans did they collect in August? _____

5 Which number could be a remainder when dividing by 4?

○ 7   ○ 2

○ 8   ○ 10

Which number could be a remainder when dividing by 8?

○ 7   ○ 16

○ 9   ○ 10

6 Write the number that is 100 less than

782,945 _____

541,099 _____

610,056 _____

7 Which number shows 6 million, 29 hundred thousands, 6 ten thousands, 1 ten, and 5 ones?

○ 6,296,150

○ 8,960,015

○ 6,290,615

○ 82,900,105

8 How many vertices are in the figures below?

_____

_____

9 Elliot has a playoff game on Saturday at 4:00. This week, he has offered to do 3 chores for his grandmother, 5 chores for his mom, and 2 chores for his dad. Each chore takes about 30 minutes. Will he have time to do all the chores and still make it to the game on time if he gets up at 10:00? _____

_____

10 Write the fraction and the decimal for each model.

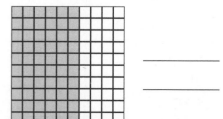
_____

_____

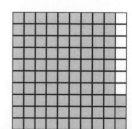
_____

_____

Day #1

Which number has a larger digit in the hundreds place than in the ten thousands place?

- ○ 3,928,743
- ○ 5,190,812
- ○ 6,278,421
- ○ 2,599,328

A square has 4 lines of symmetry

How many lines of symmetry does a hexagon have? ___

Kalyn is baking 7 batches of cookies for the church social. Each batch uses the same amount of sugar. If she uses a total of 28 cups of sugar, which expression would tell the cups of sugar needed for each batch?

- ○ 7 x 28
- ○ 28 ÷ 7
- ○ 28 + 7
- ○ 28 − 7

$$\begin{array}{r} 8,679 \\ 4,527 \\ + 6,382 \\ \hline \end{array}$$

$$\begin{array}{r} 622 \\ \times\ 52 \\ \hline \end{array}$$

Day #2

Write the decimal shown by each model.

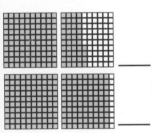

_____

_____

Which equation below best expresses the quotient for a number fact that equals 5?

- ○ 1 + 4 = 5
- ○ 25 − 20 = 5
- ○ 5 x 1 = 5
- ○ 25 ÷ 5 = 5

Mrs. Ganzer spends an hour doing laundry, 45 minutes vacuuming, a half-hour dusting, and 25 minutes mopping when she cleans house. How long does it take her to complete her housework? _____

Which series continues the pattern? _____
A. ✄♣✄

B. ★✄✌

C. ✄♣♣

Day #3

Continue counting. Write the next six numbers.

739,995
739,996
739,997
_____
_____
_____
_____
_____
_____

Find the volume for each solid figure below.

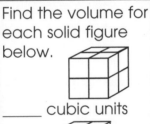

_____ cubic units

_____ cubic units

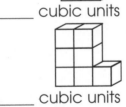

What number does the star best represent?

- ○ 12.5
- ○ 12.7
- ○ 13.5
- ○ 13.7

$8\overline{)600}$

$6\overline{)390}$

Day #4

orange = 40   green = 24
white = 16   purple = 48

To correctly color the pie graph so that it matches the above data, each section must stand for the same number. Determine that number, then color the graph.

each part

= _____

Tam's age is an even number less than 14. He is one-half his sister's age. His sister's age is a number between 16 and 24.

How old is Tam? ____

How old is his sister? _____

Casey's bead art set has 372 beads for each of 12 colors. She saw 23 more sets like hers in the craft store. Which is the best estimate for the number of beads in all the sets?

- ○ 80,000
- ○ 70,000
- ○ 60,000
- ○ 100,000

| 1 | 5 | 9 | 1 | 5 |

If these cards are shuffled and placed facedown, the chances of drawing a 1 are _____ to the chances of drawing a 5, and _____ times greater than the chances of drawing a 9.

Assessment

1

$$
\begin{array}{r}
345 \\
\times\ 47 \\
\hline
\end{array}
\qquad
\begin{array}{r}
4,254 \\
9,897 \\
+\ 6,579 \\
\hline
\end{array}
$$

2

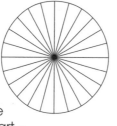

$$4\overline{)300}$$

3

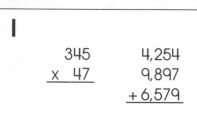

If these cards are shuffled and placed facedown, the chances of drawing an **✗** are _____ to the chances of drawing a ▲ and _____ times greater than drawing a ✓.

4

The letter A best represents what number?

- ○ 11.9
- ○ 10.5
- ○ 11.5
- ○ 10.7

5 Wayne is boxing fireworks for sale at his uncle's stand. Each box contains the same number. So far he has 210 fireworks in 7 boxes. Which expression would tell how many fireworks are in each box?

- ○ 210 + 7
- ○ 210 x 7
- ○ 210 – 7
- ○ 210 ÷ 7

6 **Artworks Exhibited at Children's Art Fairs**

1995 = 25   color white
1996 = 20   color green
1997 = 40   color blue
1998 = 35   color red

Color the pie graph to match the above data by determining the value of each section. each part = _____

7 Mindy and her friends went to the county fair. They spent 1 hour and 20 minutes riding the rides. They played games at the booths for 45 minutes, visited the exhibits for a half-hour, then went into the fun house for 15 minutes before going home. How long did Mindy and her friends stay at the fair? _____

8 Find the volume for the solid figures below.

_____ cubic units   _____ cubic units

9 Which numeral has a lesser digit in the hundred thousands place than in the tens place?

- ○ 5,836,170
- ○ 8,208,957
- ○ 6,530,659
- ○ 2,970,885

10 At the candy factory, the workers pack 47 chocolate delights in each box. They can pack about 53 boxes each hour. What is the best estimate of the number of chocolate delights packed in 8 hours?

- ○ 20,000
- ○ 21,000
- ○ 22,000
- ○ 23,000

Day #1

Which number has a lesser digit in the thousands place than in the ten millions place?

○ 347,928,743

○ 562,147,812

○ 620,213,401

○ 754,563,928

A square has 4 lines of symmetry.

How many lines of symmetry does a pentagon have?

_____

What is the difference in length between a hiking trail 20,402 meters long and a trail 13,857 meters long? _____

$$\begin{array}{r} 321 \\ \times\ 52 \\ \hline \end{array}$$

$$12\frac{15}{30}$$

$$+\ 6\frac{25}{30}$$

Day #2

Add the decimals shown by each model.

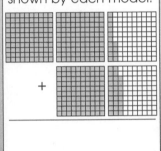

+

= _____

Tony's math grades are 85, 92, 95, 81, and 92.

What is his average grade in math? _____

How can you make $1.27 using a minimal collection of these coins?

____ nickels
____ dimes
____ pennies

How can you make $1.27 using a minimal collection of these coins?

____ quarters
____ pennies

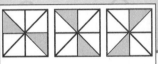

Shade in the next two squares to continue the pattern.

Day #3

Continue counting. Write the next seven numbers.
995,985
995,990
995,995

_____
_____
_____
_____
_____
_____

Find the volume for each solid figure below.

____ cubic units

____ cubic units

What number does the star best represent?

○ 13.25

○ 13.50

○ 13.75

○ 14.10

$$50\overline{)4,500}$$

$$25\frac{2}{12}$$

$$-\ 14\frac{10}{12}$$

Day #4

[grid graph with points A–F]

Name the ordered pairs.

A _____ B _____
C _____ D _____
E _____ F _____

The area of the dining table is an even number. The desk is a square. The coffee table's length is three times its width. The end table's area is one-half of one of the other tables. Match the area to each table.

6 sq. ft. _____
20 sq. ft. _____
12 sq. ft. _____
16 sq. ft. _____

33,452,835 rounded to the nearest

10 = _____

1,000 = _____

100,000 = _____

1,000,000 = _____

Subtract. Simplify the answer.

$$11\frac{3}{9} - \frac{4}{9} = \underline{\quad}$$

$$\frac{21}{5} - \frac{6}{5} = \underline{\quad}$$

$$17\frac{3}{24} - 8\frac{5}{24} = \underline{\quad}$$

Assessment

1

$$\begin{array}{r} 345 \\ \times\ 32 \end{array} \qquad 40\overline{)2,800}$$

2 Subtract and simplify the answer.

$$12\frac{3}{14} - 7\frac{10}{14} = \underline{\quad}$$

$$\frac{24}{8} - \frac{20}{8} = \underline{\quad}$$

3 6,251,481 rounded to the nearest

$$100 = \underline{\hspace{3cm}}$$

$$10,000 = \underline{\hspace{3cm}}$$

$$100,000 = \underline{\hspace{3cm}}$$

4 What is the difference in length between a highway 147,895 meters long and a highway 601,234 meters long? _____

5 What is Ray's average score in bowling? _____

Ray's Bowling Scores	
Game	Points per Game
1	102
2	98
3	129
4	201
5	80

6 Continue counting. Write the next seven numbers. _____

895,680   _____

895,780   _____

895,880   _____

895,980   _____

7 Which number has a digit of greater value in the hundred thousands place than in the ten millions place?

○ 875,836,170

○ 861,508,957

○ 651,530,659

○ 280,190,885

8 How many lines of symmetry are there for each figure?

Draw in lines of symmetry.

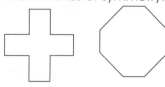

_____   _____   _____

9 How can you make $2.38 using a minimal collection of these coins? Write the amount for each coin.

quarters _____   nickels _____   pennies _____

How can you make $2.38 using a minimal collection of these coins? Write the amount for each coin.

half-dollars _____   quarters _____

dimes _____   pennies _____

10 Name the ordered pairs.

A _____

B _____

C _____

D _____

E _____

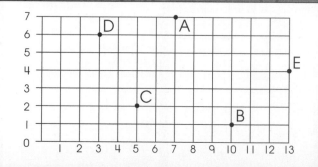

Day #1

In 1978, the most expensive coin was a $20.00 gold piece. Hal read that the gold piece sold for an approximate dollar amount that had an 8 in the tens place, a 4 in the thousands place, a 5 in the ones place, and a 3 in the hundred thousands place. What was the price of the coin? $_____.00

Label the lines I for intersecting, PA for parallel, and P for perpendicular.

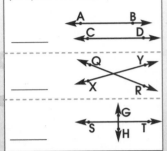

_____

_____

_____

_____

The greatest oil gusher was at Spindletop, Texas in 1901. It yielded about 810,459 barrels of oil in 9 days. About how many barrels of oil did this oil gusher produce each day?

_____

605
x 85

20)‾453‾

Day #2

Subtract the decimals shown by each model.

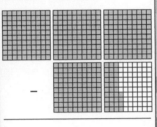

−

= _____

Circle common factors for each number pair

4, 16

2 4 8 10 16 20

10, 20

2 3 4 5 10 20

18, 36

2 3 4 6 9 12 18

Oscar earns $5.25 per hour working part time at the grocery store. Last week he worked 4 hours a day for 6 days. How much did Oscar earn last week?

_____

9, 11, 15, 23, 39, 7

What is the rule for the pattern above? (Hint: use two operations.)

_____

_____

Day #3

Japanese Cities Populations 1977

Tokyo	8,112,000
Osaka	3,276,000
Yokohama	2,601,000
Sapporo	2,162,000
Nagoya	1,719,000

List the cities in order from least to greatest population. _____

_____

_____

Using the lines of symmetry, find the perimeter of this hexagon.

2 cm
5 cm
2 cm

perimeter = _____ cm

The continent of Asia has a land mass of forty-three million, nine hundred seventy-five thousand square kilometers. This number is written in numerals as

○ 43,975,000
○ 430,975
○ 439,750,000
○ 43,975

4.37	9.82
6.22	3.41
+ 4.50	+ 7.25

| 9.82 | 8.12 |
| − 3.25 | − 6.78 |

Day #4

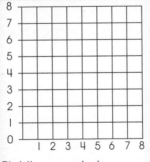

Plot these symbols.

✖ = (8, 7)   ◆ = (0, 2)
▲ = (4, 6)   ■ = (5, 1)

Popeye Pig ate over 100 peanuts, which was twice as many peanuts as Pinky Pig ate. Pinky ate a number of peanuts that is divisible by 7. Petunia Pig ate 11 more peanuts than Pinky. The number she ate is an odd number between 60 and 70. How many peanuts did each pig eat?

Popeye _____ Pinky _____
Petunia _____

The world's largest park is the Wood Buffalo Park in Canada. It is 19,362 times larger than the world's oldest park in London, which covers 577 acres. Which equation best estimates the size of the Canadian park?

○ 21,400 x 700
○ 20,000 x 500
○ 19,000 x 600
○ 20,000 x 400

$9 \frac{19}{42} + 17 \frac{25}{42} =$ _____

$52 \frac{12}{30} - 25 \frac{22}{30} =$ _____

$31 \frac{1}{15} - 18 \frac{9}{15} =$ _____

Assessment

1

$$\begin{array}{r} 403 \\ \times\ 75 \\ \hline \end{array}$$

$60\overline{)385}$

2

$$\begin{array}{r} 3.05 \\ 2.61 \\ +\ 9.85 \\ \hline \end{array}$$

$$\begin{array}{r} 12.21 \\ -\ 9.85 \\ \hline \end{array}$$

3   4, 17, 56, 173, 524

What is the rule for the pattern?

(Hint: use two operations.)

_____

4 In square miles, the country of India has an area of one million, two hundred twenty-nine thousand, seven hundred thirty-seven. This number is written

○ 12,297,037

○ 1,229,737

○ 122,973,007

5 During one week in August, the Icy Freeze Shop used 140,210 ice cubes to make snow cones. If the Icy Freeze Shop used the same number of ice cubes each day, how many ice cubes were used daily?

_____

6 Plot the symbols.

✔ = (10, 7)

✚ = (1, 8)

■ = (0, 3)

○ = (5, 5)

7 Evan spent $9.48 a week to rent videos. How much did he spend in 8 weeks? _____

8 Using the lines of symmetry, find the perimeter of this figure.

perimeter = _____ mm

5 mm
←10 mm
↓20 mm
5 mm

9 Scott was looking at a warehouse catalog for ordering music cassette tapes, compact disks, and albums. The number of items available through the catalog had a 7 in the ten thousands place, a 5 in the hundreds place, a 9 in the hundred thousands place, and a 6 in the ones place. How many items were in the catalog?

_____

10 In the 1890s, railroad passenger travel was estimated to be about 11,848,000 passenger miles. In 1974, the number of passenger miles was 67 times that amount. Which equation best estimates the number of passenger miles traveled in 1974?

○ 1,890 x 11 million

○ 60 x 11,000 million

○ 70 x 12 million

○ 60 x 10,000 million

Susan read that one of the longest toy balloon flights achieved a record length in miles. The balloon traveled an approximate distance that had a 1 in the hundreds place, a 5 in the tens place, a 9 in the thousands place, a 7 in the hundredths place, and a 5 in the tenths place. How far did the balloon travel?

_____ miles

Label each figure by drawing the letter inside the figure.
A. a pentagon with 2 right angles
B. a quadrilateral with 1 right angle
C. an equilateral triangle
D. a right triangle

One of the largest living trees, the General Sherman tree is a Sequoia in California. It is about 272.3 feet tall. The tallest redwood tree is about 367.8 feet tall. What is the difference in height between the two trees? _____

923
x 381

50)‾1,532

Day #1

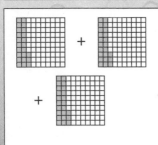

= 3 x 0.23 = _____

What is the greatest common factor for

12 and 16_____

20 and 30_____

36 and 35_____

How many?

8 hours = _____ minutes

3 days = _____ hours

1 hour = _____ seconds

one-quarter hour = _____ minutes

1 year = _____ hours

Create your own pattern.

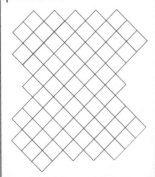

Day #2

Write the decimals in order from least to greatest.

3.45 3.5 3.82
3.02 3.1 3.67

_____, _____,

_____, _____,

_____, _____

Use the grid to enlarge the top figure to two times its size.

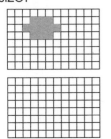

In 1970, a car, "The Blue Flame," achieved an average speed of six hundred twenty-seven and twenty-nine hundredths miles per hour. This number is written

○ 62,729.0029

○ 627.29

○ 627.029

34.97
16.2
+ 54.03

30.02
- 16.18

42.12
- 29.9

19.02
73.69
+ 13.5

Day #3

Number of Girls & Boys Enrolled at Burns Elementary School girls ▧ boys ▪

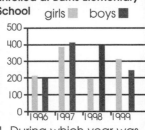

1. During which year was the enrollment for girls and boys about the same? _____

Use the graph at the left.

2. In which year was the enrollment less for girls than boys? _____

3. In which year was the enrollment for boys about 390? _____

4. In which years was the enrollment for girls about 200?

_____ _____

Aidan has 4 collections: rocks, shells, stamps, and marbles. Each collection has between 20 and 50 items. What is a reasonable total for all the items in his collections?

○ 75

○ 520

○ 150

In a meter race, Alan ran 3 times as far as Cathy. Cathy ran one-half as far as David. David's total meters run was a multiple of 7 less than 50. Becky ran 21 times less than the number of meters run by Alan. How many meters did each child run?

Alan _____
Becky _____
Cathy _____
David _____

Day #4

Assessment

1

726
x 438

80)5,625

2

71.90
36.7
+ 19.09

31.04
– 17.18

3 Emil played hoops 5 times. Each time he made between 10 and 40 baskets. What is a reasonable total for the baskets made by Emil?

○ 205   ○ 185

○ 50   ○ 20

4 In 1965, an American aviator flew his plane at speeds of about 3,331.5 kilometers per hour. In 1962, a Russian aviator flew his plane at about 2,680.00 kilometers per hour. What is the difference in speed between the two flights?

_____ kph

5 Circle the common factor for the pairs of numbers.

10, 15

2   3   5

24, 40

2   3   5   6   8   10

6 Write the decimals in order from greatest to least.

7.28   7.02   7.82   7.08   7.8   8.1

_____, _____, _____,

_____, _____, _____

7 Manuel was reading that one of the tallest structures in the world was a radio tower in Poland. The tower's height in feet has a 1 in the hundreds place, a 2 in the tens place, a 2 in the thousands place, and an 8 in the tenths place. Write the height of the building. _____

8 Label each figure. Write the label inside each figure.
A. a pentagon with 2 right angles
B. a quadrilateral with 2 right angles
C. a right triangle

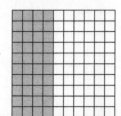

9 How many?

6 hours = _____ minutes

5 days = _____ hours

one-quarter hour = _____ minutes

1 hour = _____ seconds

10 Use the models to multiply the decimals.

  x 2 = _____

  x 5 = _____

0-7682-3204-X *Math 4 Today*

Name

Day #1

Which number has a 5 in the ten thousands place, a 3 in the hundreds place, an 8 in the millions place, and a 6 in the hundredths place?

○ 850,308.60
○ 8,005,308.30
○ 8,057,308.06
○ 85,360,016.6

Label each triangle
A. right triangle
B. scalene triangle
C. acute triangle

_____

Each student in Mr. Hernandez's class brought $3.25 for the end of the year pizza party. The party cost $78.00. What information is needed to determine whether there will be enough money? _____

_____

$$145 \times \boxed{} = 2900$$

$$\boxed{}\,\overline{)2{,}550}\;51$$

Day #2

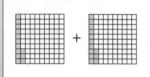

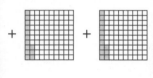

_____ x 4 = _____

If 30 is 4 times less than a number, which equation could be used to find the number?

○ 30 x 4 = n
○ 30 ÷ 4 = n
○ 30 + 4 = n
○ 30 – 4 = n

Ikito spends $4\frac{1}{2}$ hours practicing his violin each week. He has practiced for $1\frac{3}{4}$ hours this week. How many more minutes does he need to practice? _____

10	13	19	22
7	10	16	19

What two numbers are missing from this pattern?

Day #3

Write the decimals in order from greatest to least.

12.85 13.2 12.08
13.02 13.50 12.6

_____ , _____ ,

_____ , _____ ,

_____ , _____

Use the grid to enlarge the top figure three times its size.

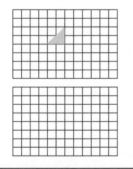

Match using the number line.

_____ 37.21

_____ 35.4

_____ 37.89

_____ 36.5

$$5{,}340 - \boxed{} = 3{,}702$$

$$9{,}846 + \boxed{} = 14{,}772$$

Day #4

Average Minutes to Complete 1K Race

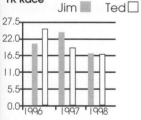

Which chart to the right best matches the data on the above graph? _____

		Jim	Ted
A	1996	20.2	25.5
	1997	24.7	20.5
	1998	19.21	18.85
B	1996	16.5	27.5
	1997	20.7	20.5
	1998	11.21	12.85
C	1996	22.0	25.5
	1997	28.7	20.5
	1998	19.21	5.85

Each year Rita has between 21 and 45 classmates. What is a reasonable total for the number of classmates she had in grades one through six?

○ 120
○ 250
○ 350

For a community food drive, Mrs. Witt needed to pack 438 cans of vegetables. She can pack 40 cans in each box. What is the fewest number of boxes she can use to pack all the cans? _____

Assessment

1

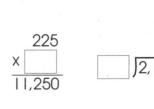

$$\begin{array}{r} 225 \\ \times \; \boxed{} \\ \hline 11,250 \end{array}$$

$$\boxed{}\,\overline{)\,2,100\,}^{\;30}$$

2

$$\begin{array}{r} 7,109 \\ - \; \boxed{} \\ \hline 4,387 \end{array}$$

$$\begin{array}{r} 8,298 \\ + \; \boxed{} \\ \hline 13,105 \end{array}$$

3

11	18	24	39
2	9	14	30

Which two numbers are missing from this pattern?

4

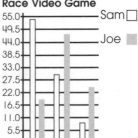

A   B   C D   E
42   43   44   45

Match using the number line.

_____ 44.10   _____ 42.92

_____ 44.5   _____ 43.75

_____ 42.25

5 Several friends went to Six Flags Amusement Park. Their total entrance fee was $264.00. What information do you need to find out the entrance fee for each person?

_____

6

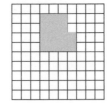

Average Miles on Road Race Video Game

Sam ☐
Joe ▨

Circle the chart that best matches the graph.

Game	1	2	3
Sam	53.5	22.1	8.79
Joe	12.3	38.2	17.5

Game	1	2	3
Sam	52.2	27.9	8.79
Joe	19.3	45.2	22.3

7 Paula's goal is to jog for 2 hours and 45 minutes a week. So far this week, she has jogged for three-quarters of an hour. How many more minutes does she need to jog to meet her weekly goal?_____

8 Use the empty grid to enlarge this shape two times.

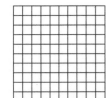

9 Which number has a 5 in the tens place, a 7 in the ten thousands place, a 6 in the millions place, and a 4 in the hundredths place?

○ 5,760,401

○ 6,270,052.04

○ 5,670,219.4

○ 6,870,059.40

10 Erin goes swimming between 52 and 105 times each summer. What would be a reasonable total of the times she has gone swimming over the last 6 years?

○ 525

○ 725

○ 825

○ 225

Answer Key

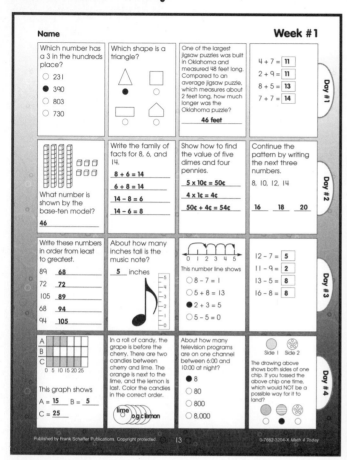

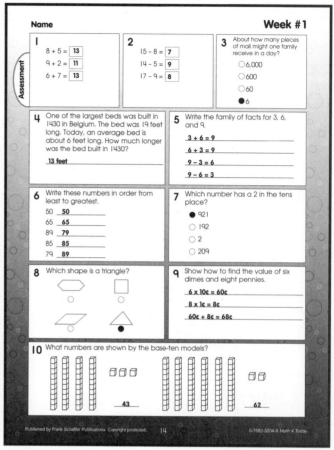

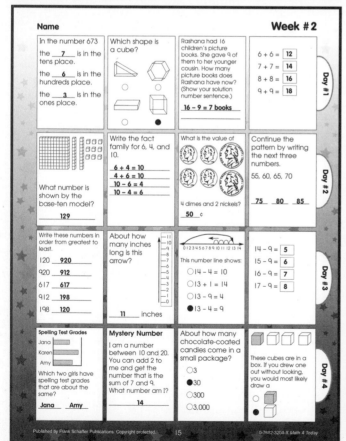

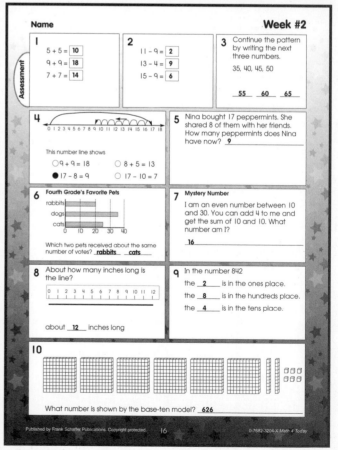

Answer Key

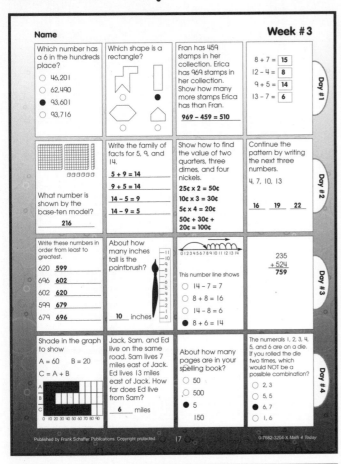

Day #1

Which number has a 6 in the hundreds place?
- ○ 46,201
- ○ 62,490
- ● 93,601
- ○ 93,716

Which shape is a rectangle?

Fran has 459 stamps in her collection. Erica has 969 stamps in her collection. Show how many more stamps Erica has than Fran.

969 − 459 = 510

8 + 7 = **15**
12 − 4 = **8**
9 + 5 = **14**
13 − 7 = **6**

Day #2

What number is shown by the base-ten model?
216

Write the family of facts for 5, 9, and 14.
5 + 9 = 14
9 + 5 = 14
14 − 5 = 9
14 − 9 = 5

Show how to find the value of two quarters, three dimes, and four nickels.
25¢ × 2 = 50¢
10¢ × 3 = 30¢
5¢ × 4 = 20¢
50¢ + 30¢ + 20¢ = 100¢

Continue the pattern by writing the next three numbers.
4, 7, 10, 13
16 19 22

Day #3

Write these numbers in order from least to greatest.
620 **599**
696 **602**
602 **620**
599 **679**
679 **696**

About how many inches tall is the paintbrush?
10 inches

This number line shows
- ○ 14 − 7 = 7
- ○ 8 + 8 = 16
- ○ 14 − 8 = 6
- ● 8 + 6 = 14

235
+ 524
759

Day #4

Shade in the graph to show
A = 60 B = 20
C = A + B

Jack, Sam, and Ed live on the same road. Sam lives 7 miles east of Jack. Ed lives 13 miles east of Jack. How far does Ed live from Sam?
6 miles

About how many pages are in your spelling book?
- ○ 50
- ○ 500
- ● 5
- ○ 150

The numerals 1, 2, 3, 4, 5, and 6 are on a die. If you rolled the die two times, which would NOT be a possible combination?
- ○ 2, 3
- ○ 5, 5
- ● 6, 7
- ○ 1, 6

Published by Frank Schaffer Publications. Copyright protected.   17   0-7682-3204-X *Math 4 Today*

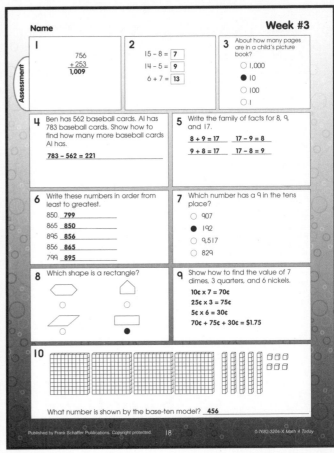

Assessment

1.
756
+ 253
1,009

2.
15 − 8 = **7**
14 − 5 = **9**
6 + 7 = **13**

3. About how many pages are in a child's picture book?
- ○ 1,000
- ● 10
- ○ 100
- ○ 1

4. Ben has 562 baseball cards. Al has 783 baseball cards. Show how to find how many more baseball cards Al has.
783 − 562 = 221

5. Write the family of facts for 8, 9, and 17.
8 + 9 = 17   **17 − 9 = 8**
9 + 8 = 17   **17 − 8 = 9**

6. Write these numbers in order from least to greatest.
850 **799**
865 **850**
895 **856**
856 **865**
799 **895**

7. Which number has a 9 in the tens place?
- ○ 907
- ● 192
- ○ 9,517
- ○ 829

8. Which shape is a rectangle?

9. Show how to find the value of 7 dimes, 3 quarters, and 6 nickels.
10¢ × 7 = 70¢
25¢ × 3 = 75¢
5¢ × 6 = 30¢
70¢ + 75¢ + 30¢ = $1.75

10. What number is shown by the base-ten model? **456**

Published by Frank Schaffer Publications. Copyright protected.   18   0-7682-3204-X *Math 4 Today*

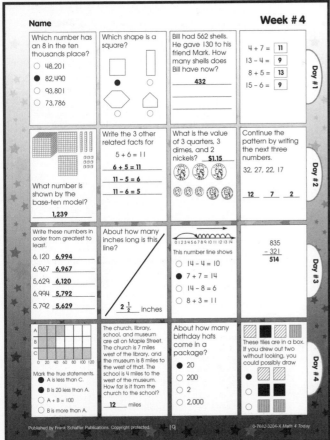

Day #1

Which number has an 8 in the ten thousands place?
- ○ 48,201
- ● 82,490
- ○ 93,801
- ○ 73,786

Which shape is a square?

Bill had 562 shells. He gave 130 to his friend Mark. How many shells does Bill have now?
432

4 + 7 = **11**
13 − 4 = **9**
8 + 5 = **13**
15 − 6 = **9**

Day #2

What number is shown by the base-ten model?
1,239

Write the 3 other related facts for
5 + 6 = 11
6 + 5 = 11
11 − 5 = 6
11 − 6 = 5

What is the value of 3 quarters, 3 dimes, and 2 nickels? **$1.15**

Continue the pattern by writing the next three numbers.
32, 27, 22, 17
12 7 2

Day #3

Write these numbers in order from greatest to least.
6,120 **6,994**
6,967 **6,967**
5,629 **6,120**
6,994 **5,792**
5,792 **5,629**

About how many inches long is this line?
2 ½ inches

This number line shows
- ○ 14 − 4 = 10
- ● 7 + 7 = 14
- ○ 14 − 8 = 6
- ○ 8 + 3 = 11

835
− 321
514

Day #4

Mark the true statements.
- ● A is less than C.
- ● B is 20 less than A.
- ○ A + B = 100
- ○ B is more than A.

The church, library, school, and museum are all on Maple Street. The church is 7 miles west of the library, and the museum is 8 miles to the west of that. The school is 4 miles to the west of the museum. How far is it from the church to the school?
12 miles

About how many birthday hats come in a package?
- ● 20
- ○ 200
- ○ 2
- ○ 2,000

These tiles are in a box. If you drew out two without looking, you could possibly draw

Published by Frank Schaffer Publications. Copyright protected.   19   0-7682-3204-X *Math 4 Today*

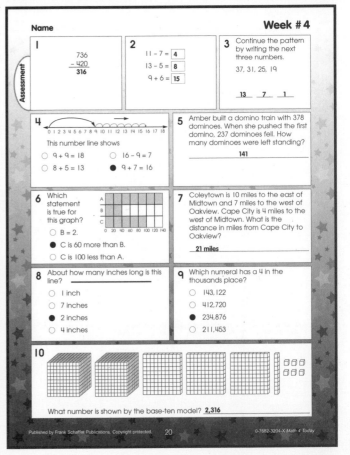

Assessment

1.
736
− 420
316

2.
11 − 7 = **4**
13 − 5 = **8**
9 + 6 = **15**

3. Continue the pattern by writing the next three numbers.
37, 31, 25, 19
13 7 1

4. This number line shows
- ○ 9 + 9 = 18
- ○ 8 + 5 = 13
- ○ 16 − 9 = 7
- ● 9 + 7 = 16

5. Amber built a domino train with 378 dominoes. When she pushed the first domino, 237 dominoes fell. How many dominoes were left standing?
141

6. Which statement is true for this graph?
- ○ B = 2.
- ● C is 60 more than B.
- ○ C is 100 less than A.

7. Coleytown is 10 miles to the east of Midtown and 7 miles to the west of Oakview. Cape City is 4 miles to the west of Midtown. What is the distance in miles from Cape City to Oakview?
21 miles

8. About how many inches long is this line? _____
- ○ 1 inch
- ○ 7 inches
- ● 2 inches
- ○ 4 inches

9. Which numeral has a 4 in the thousands place?
- ○ 143,122
- ○ 412,720
- ● 234,876
- ○ 211,453

10. What number is shown by the base-ten model? **2,316**

Published by Frank Schaffer Publications. Copyright protected.   20   0-7682-3204-X *Math 4 Today*

Answer Key

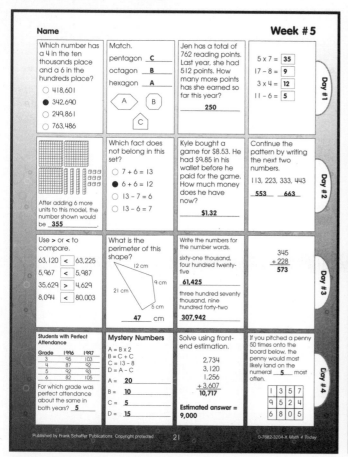

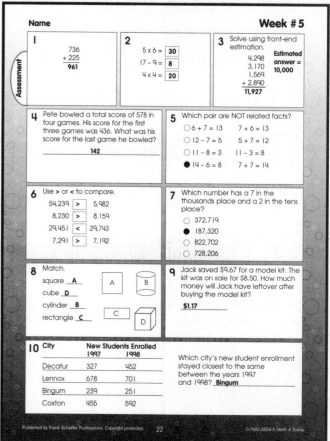

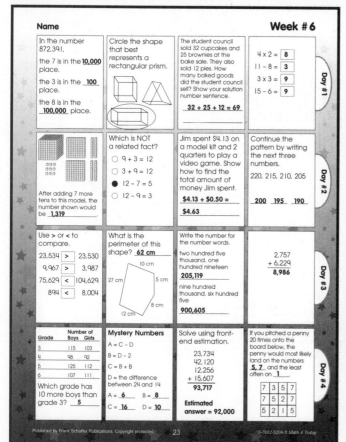

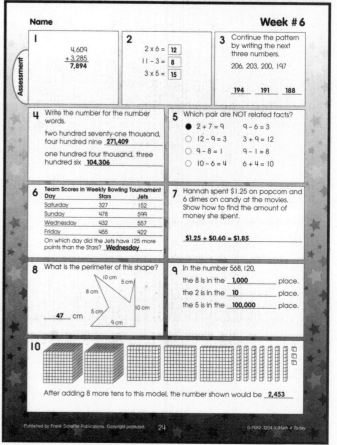

Answer Key

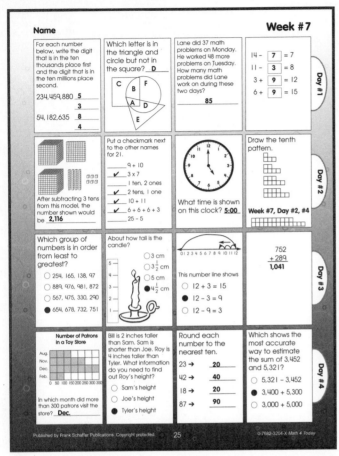

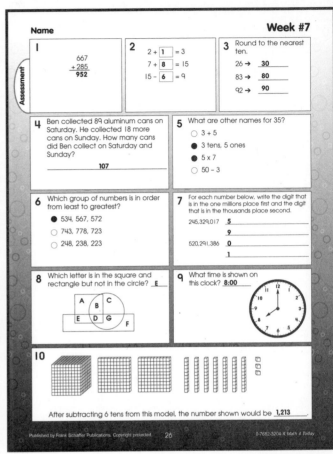

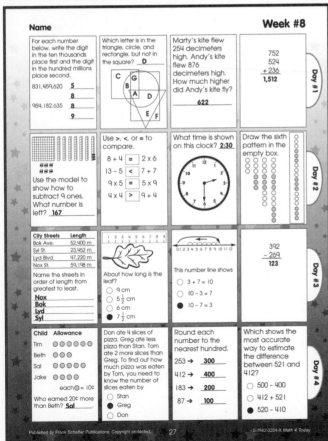

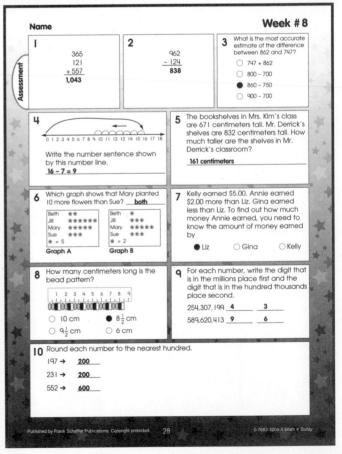

96

0-7682-3204-X *Math 4 Today*

Answer Key

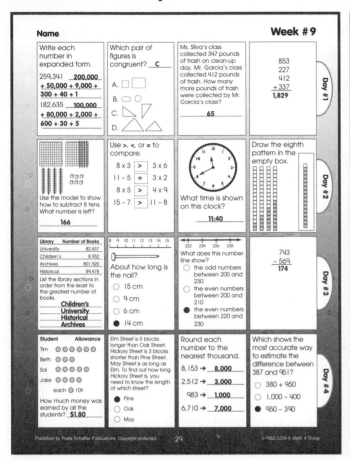

Name   **Week #9**

Write each number in expanded form.

259,341 **200,000 + 50,000 + 9,000 + 300 + 40 + 1**

182,635 **100,000 + 80,000 + 2,000 + 600 + 30 + 5**

Which pair of figures is congruent? **C**

A.
B.
C.
D.

Ms. Silva's class collected 347 pounds of trash on clean-up day. Mr. Garcia's class collected 412 pounds of trash. How many more pounds of trash were collected by Mr. Garcia's class?

65

853
227
412
+ 337
1,829

Day #1

Use the model to show how to subtract 8 tens. What number is left?

166

Use >, <, or = to compare.

8 × 3 **>** 3 × 6
11 − 5 **=** 3 × 2
8 × 5 **>** 4 × 9
15 − 7 **>** 11 − 8

What time is shown on this clock? **11:40**

Draw the eighth pattern in the empty box.

Day #2

Library	Number of Books
University	82,437
Children's	8,932
Archives	801,920
Historical	89,478

List the library sections in order from the least to the greatest number of books.
Children's
University
Historical
Archives

About how long is the nail?
○ 15 cm
○ 9 cm
○ 6 cm
● 14 cm

What does this number line show?
○ the odd numbers between 200 and 230
○ the even numbers between 200 and 210
● the even numbers between 220 and 230

743
− 569
174

Day #3

Student	Allowance
Tim	●●●●●
Beth	●●●
Sal	●●●●●
Jake	●●●

each ● 10¢

How much money was earned by all the students? **$1.80**

Elm Street is 5 blocks longer than Oak Street. Hickory Street is 3 blocks shorter than Pine Street. May Street is as long as Elm. To find out how long Hickory Street is, you need to know the length of which street?
● Pine
○ Oak
○ May

Round each number to the nearest thousand.
8,153 → **8,000**
2,512 → **3,000**
983 → **1,000**
6,710 → **7,000**

Which shows the most accurate way to estimate the difference between 387 and 951?
○ 380 + 950
○ 1,000 − 400
● 950 − 390

Day #4

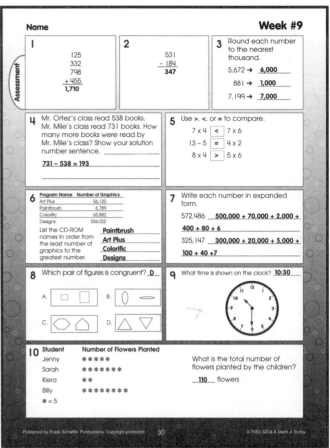

Name   **Week #9**

Assessment

1
125
332
798
+ 455
1,710

2
531
− 184
347

3 Round each number to the nearest thousand.
5,672 → **6,000**
881 → **1,000**
7,199 → **7,000**

4 Mr. Ortez's class read 538 books. Mr. Mile's class read 731 books. How many more books were read by Mr. Mile's class? Show your solution number sentence. _____
731 − 538 = 193

5 Use >, <, or = to compare.
7 × 4 **<** 7 × 6
13 − 5 **=** 4 × 2
8 × 4 **>** 5 × 6

6
Program Name	Number of Graphics
Art Plus	56,120
Paintbrush	6,789
Colorific	65,882
Designs	556,022

List the CD-ROM names in order from the least number of graphics to the greatest number.
Paintbrush
Art Plus
Colorific
Designs

7 Write each number in expanded form.
572,486 **500,000 + 70,000 + 2,000 + 400 + 80 + 6**
325,147 **300,000 + 20,000 + 5,000 + 100 + 40 + 7**

8 Which pair of figures is congruent? **D**
A.   B.   C.   D.

9 What time is shown on the clock? **10:30**

10
Student	Number of Flowers Planted
Jenny	★★★★★
Sarah	★★★★★★★
Kiera	★★
Billy	★★★★★★★★

★ = 5

What is the total number of flowers planted by the children?
110 flowers

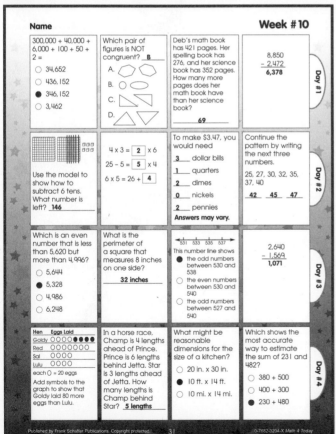

Name   **Week #10**

300,000 + 40,000 + 6,000 + 100 + 50 + 2 =
○ 34,652
○ 436,152
● 346,152
○ 3,462

Which pair of figures is NOT congruent? **B**
A.   B.   C.   D.

Deb's math book has 421 pages. Her spelling book has 276, and her science book has 352 pages. How many more pages does her math book have than her science book?
69

8,850
− 2,472
6,378

Day #1

Use the model to show how to subtract 6 tens. What number is left? **146**

4 × 3 = **2** × 6
25 − 5 = **5** × 4
6 × 5 = 26 + **4**

To make $3.47, you would need
3 dollar bills
1 quarters
2 dimes
0 nickels
2 pennies
Answers may vary.

Continue the pattern by writing the next three numbers.
25, 27, 30, 32, 35, 37, 40
42 **45** **47**

Day #2

Which is an even number that is less than 5,620 but more than 4,996?
○ 5,644
● 5,328
○ 4,986
○ 6,248

What is the perimeter of a square that measures 8 inches on one side?
32 inches

This number line shows
● the odd numbers between 530 and 538
○ the even numbers between 530 and 540
○ the odd numbers between 527 and 540

2,640
− 1,569
1,071

Day #3

Hen	Eggs Laid
Goldy	○○○○●●●●
Red	○○○○○○○
Sal	○○○○
Lulu	○○○○

each ○ = 20 eggs

Add symbols to the graph to show that Goldy laid 80 more eggs than Lulu.

In a horse race, Champ is 4 lengths ahead of Prince. Prince is 6 lengths behind Jetta. Star is 3 lengths ahead of Jetta. How many lengths is Champ behind Star? **5 lengths**

What might be reasonable dimensions for the size of a kitchen?
○ 20 in. x 30 in.
● 10 ft. x 14 ft.
○ 10 mi. x 14 mi.

Which shows the most accurate way to estimate the sum of 231 and 482?
○ 380 + 500
○ 400 + 300
● 230 + 480

Day #4

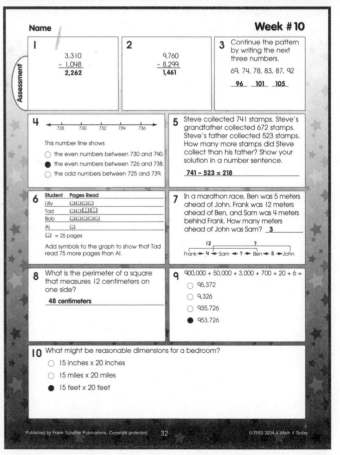

Name   **Week #10**

Assessment

1
3,310
− 1,048
2,262

2
9,760
− 8,299
1,461

3 Continue the pattern by writing the next three numbers.
69, 74, 78, 83, 87, 92
96 **101** **105**

4
728 730 732 734 736

This number line shows
○ the even numbers between 730 and 740.
● the even numbers between 726 and 738.
○ the odd numbers between 725 and 739.

5 Steve collected 741 stamps. Steve's grandfather collected 672 stamps. Steve's father collected 523 stamps. How many more stamps did Steve collect than his father? Show your solution in a number sentence.
741 − 523 = 218

6
Student	Pages Read
Lilly	▭▭▭▭
Tad	▭▭▭▭
Bob	▭▭▭▭▭
Al	▭

▭ = 25 pages

Add symbols to the graph to show that Tad read 75 more pages than Al.

7 In a marathon race, Ben was 5 meters ahead of John. Frank was 12 meters ahead of Ben, and Sam was 4 meters behind Frank. How many meters ahead of John was Sam? **3**

8 What is the perimeter of a square that measures 12 centimeters on one side?
48 centimeters

9 900,000 + 50,000 + 3,000 + 700 + 20 + 6 =
○ 95,372
○ 9,326
○ 935,726
● 953,726

10 What might be reasonable dimensions for a bedroom?
○ 15 inches x 20 inches
○ 15 miles x 20 miles
● 15 feet x 20 feet

Answer Key

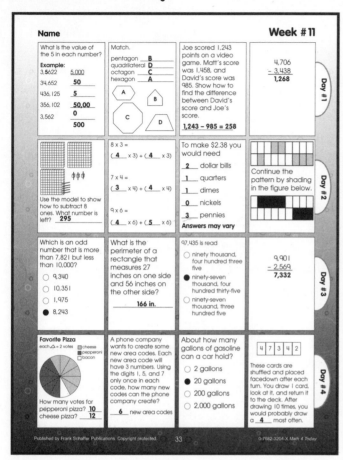

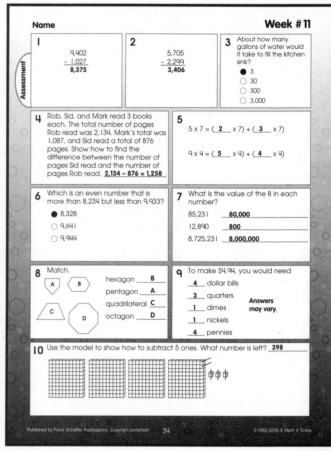

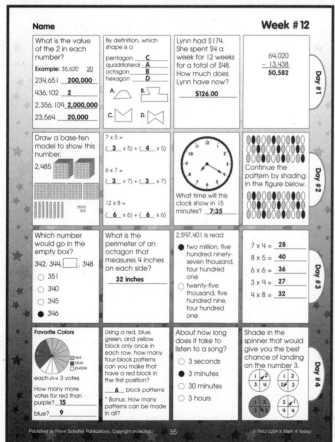

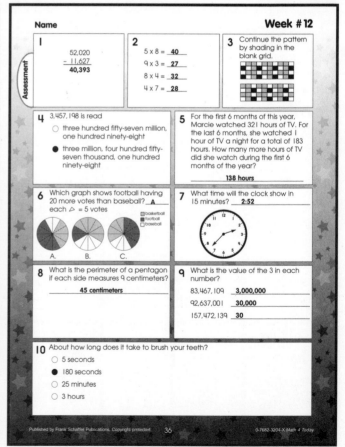

Answer Key

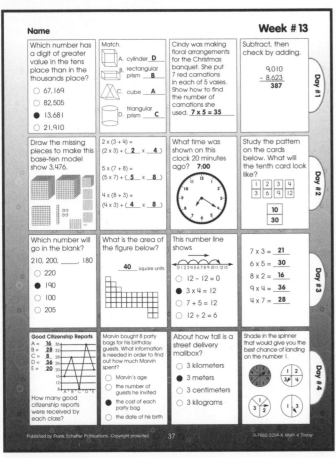

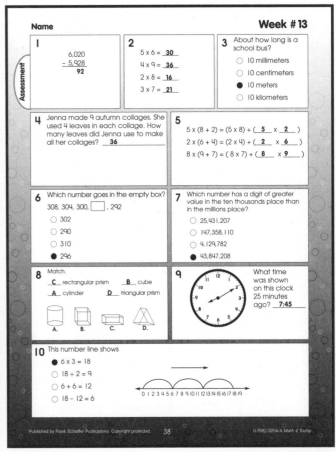

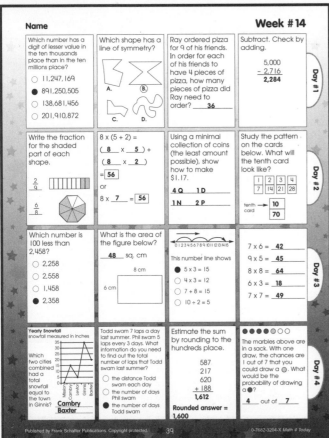

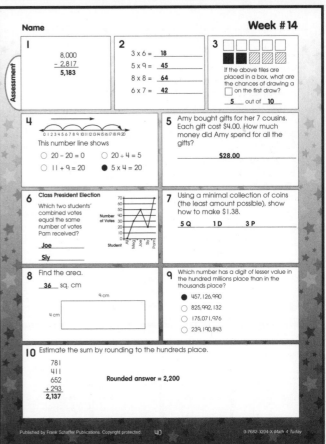

Answer Key

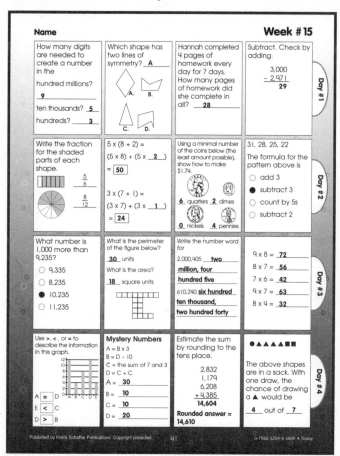

Name — **Week #15**

Day #1

How many digits are needed to create a number in the hundred millions? **9**

ten thousands? **5**

hundreds? **3**

Which shape has two lines of symmetry? **A**

A. B. C. D.

Hannah completed 4 pages of homework every day for 7 days. How many pages of homework did she complete in all? **28**

Subtract. Check by adding.
3,000
− 2,971
29

Day #2

Write the fraction for the shaded parts of each shape.
5/6
8/12

5 × (8 + 2) =
(5 × 8) + (5 × **2**) =
50

3 × (7 + 1) =
(3 × 7) + (3 × **1**)
= **24**

Using a minimal number of the coins below (the least amount possible), show how to make $1.74.
6 quarters **2** dimes
0 nickels **4** pennies

31, 28, 25, 22
The formula for the pattern above is
○ add 3
● subtract 3
○ count by 5s
○ subtract 2

Day #3

What number is 1,000 more than 9,235?
○ 9,335
○ 8,235
● 10,235
○ 11,235

What is the perimeter of the figure below? **30** units
What is the area? **18** square units

Write the number word for
2,000,405 **two million, four hundred five**
610,240 **six hundred ten thousand, two hundred forty**

9 × 8 = **72**
8 × 7 = **56**
7 × 6 = **42**
9 × 7 = **63**
8 × 4 = **32**

Day #4

Use >, <, or = to describe the information in this graph.

A = D
E < C
D > B

Mystery Numbers
A = B × 3
B = D − 10
C = the sum of 7 and 3
D = C + C
A = **30**
B = **10**
C = **10**
D = **20**

Estimate the sum by rounding to the tens place.
2,832
1,179
6,208
+ 4,385
14,604
Rounded answer = 14,610

●▲▲▲▲■■
The above shapes are in a sack. With one draw, the chance of drawing a ▲ would be **4** out of **7**

Published by Frank Schaffer Publications. Copyright protected.   41   0-7682-3204-X *Math 4 Today*

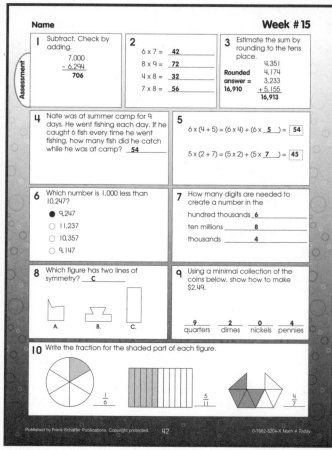

Name — **Week #15**

Assessment

1 Subtract. Check by adding.
7,000
− 6,294
706

2
6 × 7 = **42**
8 × 9 = **72**
4 × 8 = **32**
7 × 8 = **56**

3 Estimate the sum by rounding to the tens place.
4,351
4,174
3,233
+ 5,155
16,913
Rounded answer = 16,910

4 Nate was at summer camp for 9 days. He went fishing each day. If he caught 6 fish every time he went fishing, how many fish did he catch while he was at camp? **54**

5
6 × (4 + 5) = (6 × 4) + (6 × **5**) = **54**
5 × (2 + 7) = (5 × 2) + (5 × **7**) = **45**

6 Which number is 1,000 less than 10,247?
● 9,247
○ 11,237
○ 10,357
○ 9,147

7 How many digits are needed to create a number in the
hundred thousands **6**
ten millions **8**
thousands **4**

8 Which figure has two lines of symmetry? **C**
A. B. C.

9 Using a minimal collection of the coins below, show how to make $2.49.
9 quarters **2** dimes **0** nickels **4** pennies

10 Write the fraction for the shaded part of each figure.
1/6   **5/11**   **4/7**

Published by Frank Schaffer Publications. Copyright protected.   42   0-7682-3204-X *Math 4 Today*

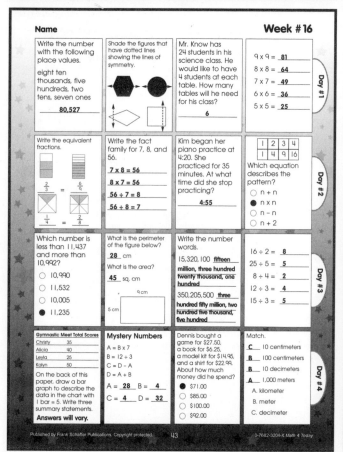

Name — **Week #16**

Day #1

Write the number with the following place values.
eight ten thousands, five hundreds, two tens, seven ones
80,527

Shade the figures that have dotted lines showing the lines of symmetry.

Mr. Know has 24 students in his science class. He would like to have 4 students at each table. How many tables will he need for his class?
6

9 × 9 = **81**
8 × 8 = **64**
7 × 7 = **49**
6 × 6 = **36**
5 × 5 = **25**

Day #2

Write the equivalent fractions.
2/3 = **6/9**
1/4 = **2/8**

Write the fact family for 7, 8, and 56.
7 × 8 = 56
8 × 7 = 56
56 ÷ 7 = 8
56 ÷ 8 = 7

Kim began her piano practice at 4:20. She practiced for 35 minutes. At what time did she stop practicing?
4:55

1 2 3 4
1 4 9 16
Which equation describes the pattern?
○ n + n
● n × n
○ n − n
○ n + 2

Day #3

Which number is less than 11,437 and more than 10,992?
○ 10,990
○ 11,532
○ 10,005
● 11,235

What is the perimeter of the figure below? **28** cm
What is the area? **45** sq. cm
9 cm
5 cm

Write the number words.
15,320,100 **fifteen million, three hundred twenty thousand, one hundred**
350,205,500 **three hundred fifty million, two hundred five thousand, five hundred**

16 ÷ 2 = **8**
25 ÷ 5 = **5**
8 ÷ 4 = **2**
12 ÷ 3 = **4**
15 ÷ 3 = **5**

Day #4

Gymnastic Meet Total Scores
Christy	35
Alicia	40
Leyla	35
Kalyn	50

On the back of this paper, draw a bar graph to describe the data in the chart with 1 bar = 5. Write three summary statements. **Answers will vary.**

Mystery Numbers
A = B × 7
B = 12 ÷ 3
C = D − A
D = A + B
A = **28**   B = **4**
C = **4**   D = **32**

Dennis bought a game for $27.50, a book for $6.25, a model kit for $14.95, and a shirt for $22.99. About how much money did he spend?
● $71.00
○ $85.00
○ $100.00
○ $92.00

Match.
C 10 centimeters
B 100 centimeters
B 10 decimeters
A 1,000 meters
A. kilometer
B. meter
C. decimeter

Published by Frank Schaffer Publications. Copyright protected.   43   0-7682-3204-X *Math 4 Today*

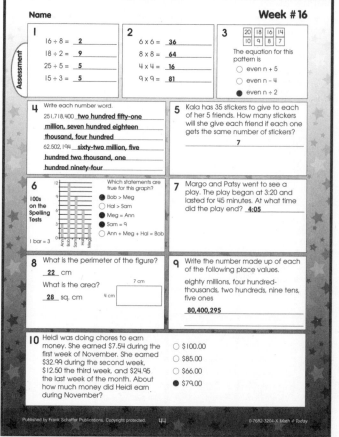

Name — **Week #16**

Assessment

1
16 ÷ 8 = **2**
18 ÷ 2 = **9**
25 ÷ 5 = **5**
15 ÷ 3 = **5**

2
6 × 6 = **36**
8 × 8 = **64**
4 × 4 = **16**
9 × 9 = **81**

3
20 18 16 14
10 9 8 7
The equation for this pattern is
○ even n + 5
○ even n − 4
● even n ÷ 2

4 Write each number word.
251,718,400 **two hundred fifty-one million, seven hundred eighteen thousand, four hundred**
62,502,194 **sixty-two million, five hundred two thousand, one hundred ninety-four**

5 Kala has 35 stickers to give to each of her 5 friends. How many stickers will she give each friend if each one gets the same number of stickers?
7

6
100s on the Spelling Tests
1 bar = 3
Which statements are true for this graph?
● Bob > Meg
○ Hal > Sam
● Meg > Ann
○ Sam = 9
○ Ann + Meg + Hal > Bob

7 Margo and Patsy went to see a play. The play began at 3:20 and lasted for 45 minutes. At what time did the play end? **4:05**

8 What is the perimeter of the figure? **22** cm
What is the area? **28** sq. cm
7 cm
4 cm

9 Write the number made up of each of the following place values.
eighty millions, four hundred-thousands, two hundreds, nine tens, five ones
80,400,295

10 Heidi was doing chores to earn money. She earned $7.54 during the first week of November. She earned $32.99 during the second week, $12.50 the third week, and $24.95 the last week of the month. About how much money did Heidi earn during November?
○ $100.00
○ $85.00
○ $66.00
● $79.00

Published by Frank Schaffer Publications. Copyright protected.   44   0-7682-3204-X *Math 4 Today*

Answer Key

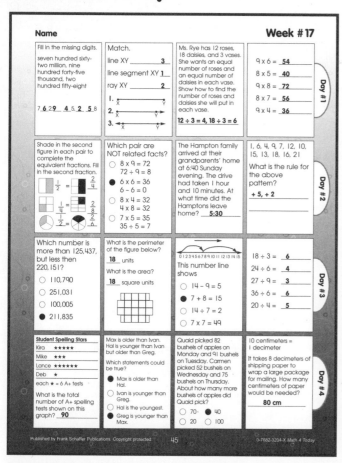

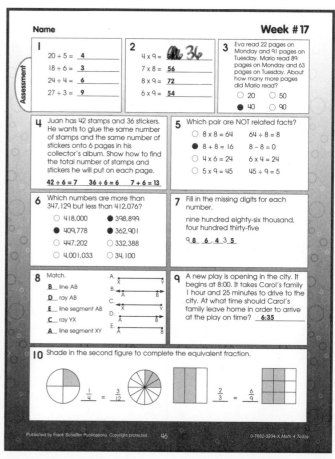

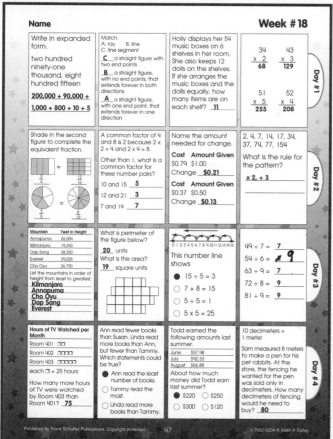

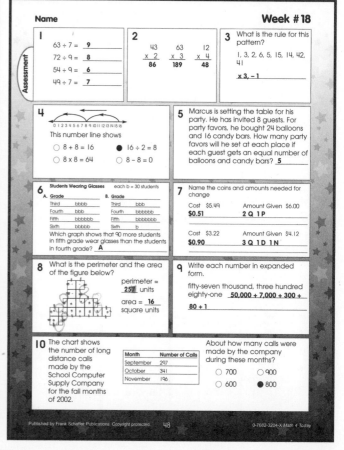

Answer Key

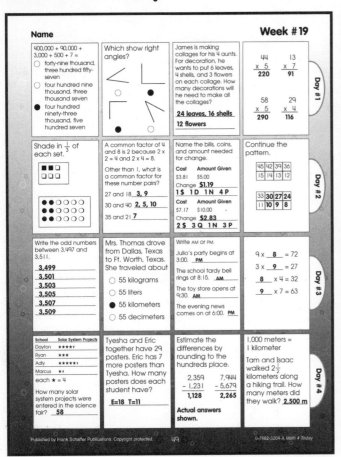

Name — Week #19

Day #1

400,000 + 90,000 + 3,000 + 500 + 7 =
○ forty-nine thousand, three hundred fifty-seven
○ four hundred nine thousand, three thousand seven
● four hundred ninety-three thousand, five hundred seven

Which show right angles?

James is making collages for his 4 aunts. For decoration, he wants to put 6 leaves, 4 shells, and 3 flowers on each collage. How many decorations will he need to make all the collages?
24 leaves, 16 shells
12 flowers

44 × 5 = **220**   13 × 7 = **91**
58 × 5 = **290**   29 × 4 = **116**

Day #2

Shade in $\frac{1}{3}$ of each set.

A common factor of 4 and 8 is 2 because 2 × 2 = 4 and 2 × 4 = 8.
Other than 1, what is a common factor for these number pairs?
27 and 18 **3, 9**
30 and 40 **2, 5, 10**
35 and 21 **7**

Name the bills, coins, and amount needed for change.
Cost $3.81 Amount Given $5.00
Change **$1.19**
1$ 1D 1N 4P
Cost $7.17 Amount Given $10.00
Change **$2.83**
2$ 3Q 1N 3P

Continue the pattern.
45 42 39 36
15 14 13 12
33 30 27 24
11 10 9 8

Day #3

Write the odd numbers between 3,497 and 3,511.
3,499
3,501
3,503
3,505
3,507
3,509

Mrs. Thomas drove from Dallas, Texas to Ft. Worth, Texas. She traveled about
○ 55 kilograms
○ 55 liters
● 55 kilometers
○ 55 decimeters

Write AM or PM.
Julio's party begins at 3:00. **PM**
The school tardy bell rings at 8:15. **AM**
The toy store opens at 9:30. **AM**
The evening news comes on at 6:00. **PM**

9 × **8** = 72
3 × **9** = 27
8 × 4 = 32
9 × 7 = 63

Day #4

School	Solar System Projects
Dayton	★★★★↑
Ryan	★★★
Adly	★★★★★★↑
Marcus	★↑

each ★ = 4

How many solar system projects were entered in the science fair? **58**

Tyesha and Eric together have 29 posters. Eric has 7 more posters than Tyesha. How many posters does each student have?
E=18 T=11

Estimate the differences by rounding to the hundreds place.
2,359 − 1,231 = **1,128**
7,944 − 5,679 = **2,265**
Actual answers shown.

1,000 meters = 1 kilometer
Tam and Isaac walked $2\frac{1}{2}$ kilometers along a hiking trail. How many meters did they walk? **2,500 m**

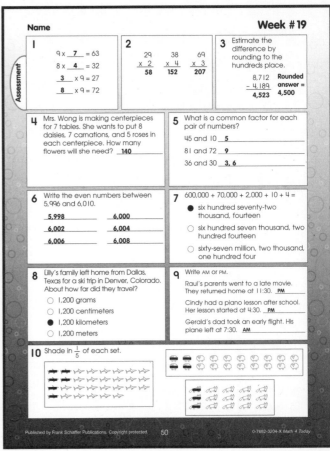

Name — Week #19

Assessment

1
9 × **7** = 63
8 × **4** = 32
3 × 9 = 27
8 × 9 = 72

2
29 × 2 = **58**
38 × 4 = **152**
69 × 3 = **207**

3 Estimate the difference by rounding to the hundreds place.
8,712 − 4,189
Rounded answer = **4,500**
4,523

4 Mrs. Wong is making centerpieces for 7 tables. She wants to put 8 daisies, 7 carnations, and 5 roses in each centerpiece. How many flowers will she need? **140**

5 What is a common factor for each pair of numbers?
45 and 10 **5**
81 and 72 **9**
36 and 30 **3, 6**

6 Write the even numbers between 5,996 and 6,010.
5,998   **6,000**
6,002   **6,004**
6,006   **6,008**

7 600,000 + 70,000 + 2,000 + 10 + 4 =
● six hundred seventy-two thousand, fourteen
○ six hundred seven thousand, two hundred fourteen
○ sixty-seven million, two thousand, one hundred four

8 Lilly's family left home from Dallas, Texas for a ski trip in Denver, Colorado. About how far did they travel?
○ 1,200 grams
○ 1,200 centimeters
● 1,200 kilometers
○ 1,200 meters

9 Write AM or PM.
Raul's parents went to a late movie. They returned home at 11:30. **PM**
Cindy had a piano lesson after school. Her lesson started at 4:30. **PM**
Gerald's dad took an early flight. His plane left at 7:30. **AM**

10 Shade in $\frac{1}{5}$ of each set.

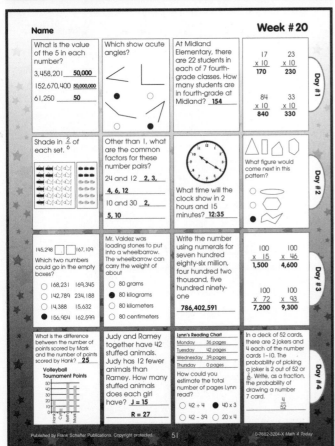

Name — Week #20

Day #1

What is the value of the 5 in each number?
3,458,201 **50,000**
152,670,400 **50,000,000**
61,250 **50**

Which show acute angles?

At Midland Elementary, there are 22 students in each of 7 fourth-grade classes. How many students are in fourth-grade at Midland? **154**

17 × 10 = **170**   23 × 10 = **230**
84 × 10 = **840**   33 × 10 = **330**

Day #2

Shade in $\frac{2}{6}$ of each set.

Other than 1, what are the common factors for these number pairs?
24 and 12 **2, 3, 4, 6, 12**
10 and 30 **2, 5, 10**

What time will the clock show in 2 hours and 15 minutes? **12:35**

What figure would come next in this pattern?

Day #3

145,298 [ ] 167,109
Which two numbers could go in the empty boxes?
○ 168,231 169,345
○ 142,789 234,188
○ 14,388 15,632
● 156,954 162,599

Mr. Valdez was loading stones to put into a wheelbarrow. The wheelbarrow can carry the weight of about
○ 80 grams
● 80 kilograms
○ 80 kilometers
○ 80 centimeters

Write the number using numerals for seven hundred eighty-six million, four hundred two thousand, five hundred ninety-one.
786,402,591

100 × 15 = **1,500**   100 × 46 = **4,600**
100 × 72 = **7,200**   100 × 93 = **9,300**

Day #4

What is the difference between the number of points scored by Mark and the number of points scored by Hank? **25**

Volleyball Tournament Points

Judy and Ramey together have 42 stuffed animals. Judy has 12 fewer animals than Ramey. How many stuffed animals does each girl have?
J = 15
R = 27

Lynn's Reading Chart
Monday **36 pages**
Tuesday **42 pages**
Wednesday **34 pages**
Thursday **0 pages**
How could you estimate the total number of pages Lynn read?
○ 42 ÷ 4 ● 40 × 3
○ 42 − 39 ○ 20 × 4

In a deck of 52 cards, there are 2 jokers and 4 each of the number cards 1–10. The probability of picking a joker is 2 out of 52 or $\frac{2}{52}$. Write, as a fraction, the probability of drawing a number 7 card. $\frac{4}{52}$

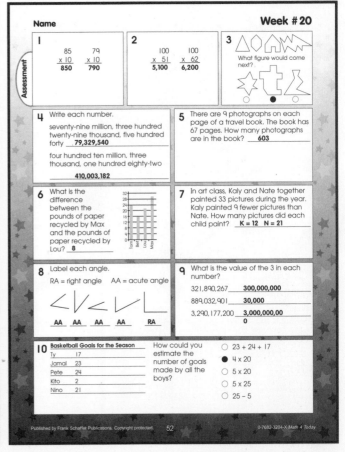

Name — Week #20

Assessment

1
85 × 10 = **850**   79 × 10 = **790**
84 × 10 = **840**?
100 × 51 = **5,100**   100 × 62 = **6,200**

2
100 × 51 = **5,100**   100 × 62 = **6,200**

3 What figure would come next?

4 Write each number.
seventy-nine million, three hundred twenty-nine thousand, five hundred forty **79,329,540**
four hundred ten million, three thousand, one hundred eighty-two **410,003,182**

5 There are 9 photographs on each page of a travel book. The book has 67 pages. How many photographs are in the book? **603**

6 What is the difference between the pounds of paper recycled by Max and the pounds of paper recycled by Lou? **8**

7 In art class, Kaly and Nate together painted 33 pictures during the year. Kaly painted 9 fewer pictures than Nate. How many pictures did each child paint? **K = 12   N = 21**

8 Label each angle.
RA = right angle   AA = acute angle
AA   AA   AA   AA   RA

9 What is the value of the 3 in each number?
321,890,267 **300,000,000**
889,032,901 **30,000**
3,290,177,200 **3,000,000,000**

10
Basketball Goals for the Season	
Ty	17
Jamal	23
Pete	24
Kito	2
Nino	21

How could you estimate the number of goals made by all the boys?
○ 23 + 24 + 17
● 4 × 20
○ 5 × 20
○ 5 × 25
○ 25 − 5

Answer Key

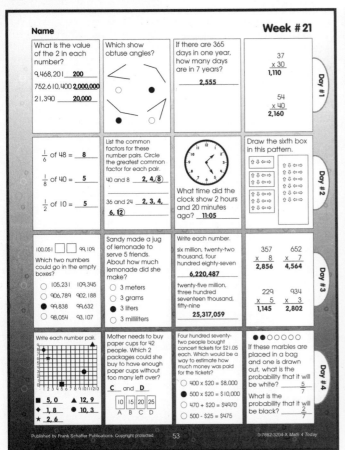

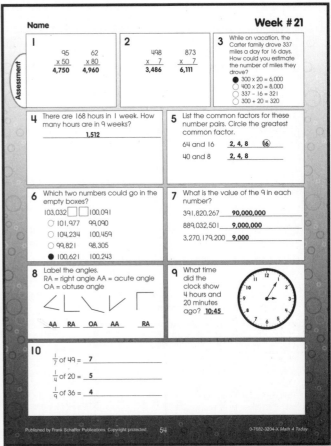

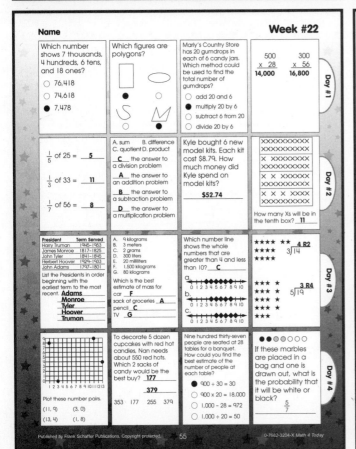

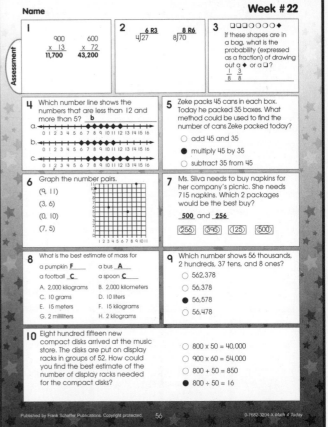

0-7682-3204-X *Math 4 Today*

Answer Key

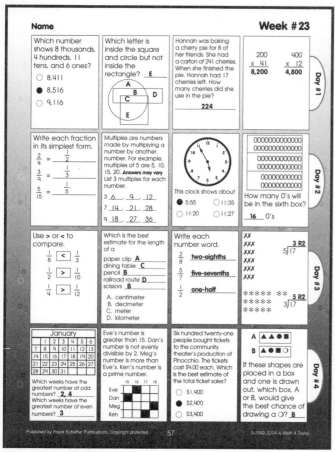

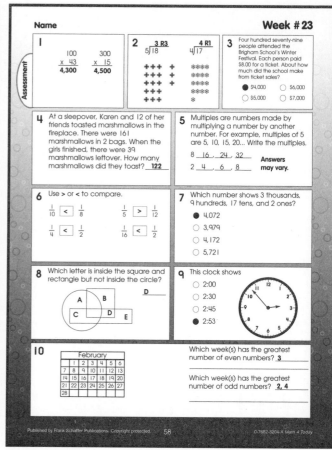

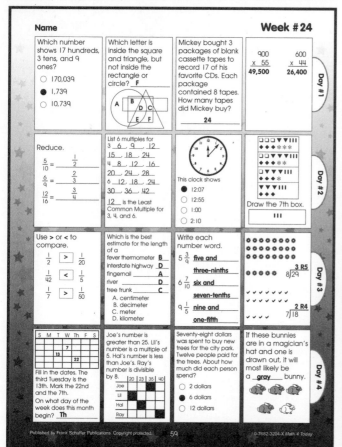

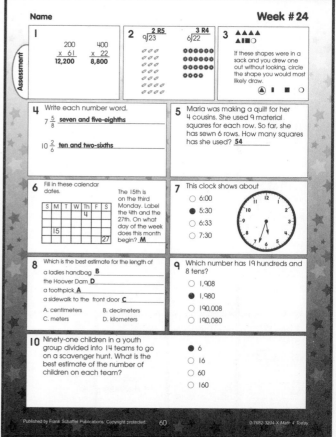

Answer Key

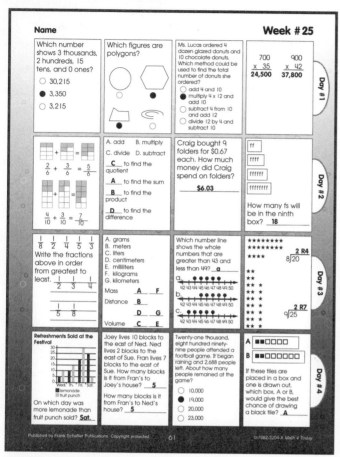

Week #25 (page 61)

Day #1

Which number shows 3 thousands, 2 hundreds, 15 tens, and 0 ones?
- ○ 30,215
- ● 3,350
- ○ 3,215

Which figures are polygons?

Ms. Lucas ordered 4 dozen glazed donuts and 10 chocolate donuts. Which method could be used to find the total number of donuts she ordered?
- ○ add 4 and 10
- ● multiply 4 x 12 and add 10
- ○ subtract 4 from 10 and add 12
- ○ divide 12 by 4 and subtract 10

$700 \times 35 = 24,500$ $900 \times 42 = 37,800$

Day #2

$\frac{2}{6} + \frac{3}{6} = \frac{5}{6}$ $\frac{4}{10} + \frac{3}{10} = \frac{7}{10}$

A. add   B. multiply
C. divide   D. subtract

C to find the quotient
A to find the sum
B to find the product
D to find the difference

Craig bought 9 folders for $0.67 each. How much money did Craig spend on folders? **$6.03**

How many fs will be in the ninth box? **18**

Day #3

$\frac{1}{8} \frac{1}{2} \frac{1}{4} \frac{1}{5} \frac{1}{3}$
Write the fractions above in order from greatest to least. $\frac{1}{2} \frac{1}{3} \frac{1}{4}$ $\frac{1}{5} \frac{1}{8}$

A. grams B. meters C. liters D. centimeters E. milliliters F. kilograms G. kilometers

Mass **A F**
Distance **B D G**
Volume **C E**

Which number line shows the whole numbers that are greater than 43 and less than 49? **a**

$8)\overline{20}$ = 2 R4
$9)\overline{25}$ = 2 R7

Day #4

Refreshments Sold at the Festival
On which day was more lemonade than fruit punch sold? **Sat.**

Joey lives 10 blocks to the east of Ned. Ned lives 2 blocks to the east of Sue. Fran lives 7 blocks to the east of Sue. How many blocks is it from Fran's to Joey's house? **5**
How many blocks is it from Fran's to Ned's house? **5**

Twenty-one thousand, eight hundred ninety-nine people attended a football game. It began raining and 2,688 people left. About how many people remained at the game?
- ○ 10,000
- ● 19,000
- ○ 20,000
- ○ 23,000

If these tiles are placed in a box and one is drawn out, which box, A or B, would give the best chance of drawing a black tile? **A**

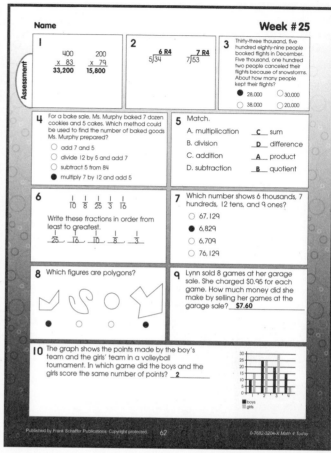

Week #25 (page 62) — Assessment

1. $400 \times 83 = 33,200$ $200 \times 79 = 15,800$

2. $5)\overline{34}$ = 6 R4 $7)\overline{53}$ = 7 R4

3. Thirty-three thousand, five hundred eighty-nine people booked flights in December. Five thousand, one hundred two people canceled their flights because of snowstorms. About how many people kept their flights?
- ● 28,000
- ○ 30,000
- ○ 38,000
- ○ 20,000

4. For a bake sale, Ms. Murphy baked 7 dozen cookies and 5 cakes. Which method could be used to find the number of baked goods Ms. Murphy prepared?
- ○ add 7 and 5
- ○ divide 12 by 5 and add 7
- ○ subtract 5 from 84
- ● multiply 7 by 12 and add 5

5. Match.
A. multiplication **C** sum
B. division **D** difference
C. addition **A** product
D. subtraction **B** quotient

6. $\frac{1}{10} \frac{1}{8} \frac{1}{25} \frac{1}{3} \frac{1}{16}$
Write these fractions in order from least to greatest. $\frac{1}{25} \frac{1}{16} \frac{1}{10} \frac{1}{8} \frac{1}{3}$

7. Which number shows 6 thousands, 7 hundreds, 12 tens, and 9 ones?
- ○ 67,129
- ● 6,829
- ○ 6,709
- ○ 76,129

8. Which figures are polygons?

9. Lynn sold 8 games at her garage sale. She charged $0.95 for each game. How much money did she make by selling her games at the garage sale? **$7.60**

10. The graph shows the points made by the boy's team and the girls' team in a volleyball tournament. In which game did the boys and the girls score the same number of points? **2**

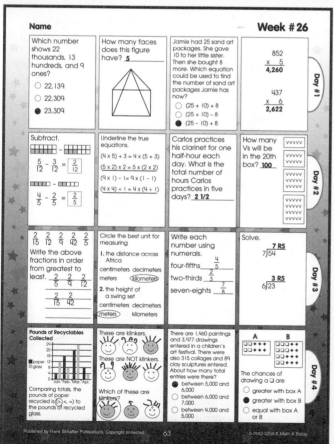

Week #26 (page 63)

Day #1

Which number shows 22 thousands, 13 hundreds, and 9 ones?
- ○ 22,139
- ○ 22,309
- ● 23,309

How many faces does this figure have? **5**

Jamie had 25 sand art packages. She gave 10 to her little sister. Then she bought 8 more. Which equation could be used to find the number of sand art packages Jamie has now?
- ○ (25 + 10) + 8
- ○ (25 + 10) – 8
- ● (25 – 10) + 8

$852 \times 5 = 4,260$
$437 \times 6 = 2,622$

Day #2

Subtract.
$\frac{5}{12} - \frac{3}{12} = \frac{2}{12}$
$\frac{4}{5} - \frac{2}{5} = \frac{2}{5}$

Underline the true equations.
(4 x 5) + 3 = 4 x (5 + 3)
(5 x 2) x 2 = 5 x (2 x 2)
(9 x 1) – 1 = 9 x (1 – 1)
(4 x 4) ÷ 1 = 4 x (4 ÷ 1)

Carlos practices his clarinet for one half-hour each day. What is the total number of hours Carlos practices in five days? **2 1/2**

How many Vs will be in the 20th box? **100**

Day #3

$\frac{2}{15} \frac{2}{9} \frac{2}{12} \frac{2}{42} \frac{2}{5}$
Write the above fractions in order from greatest to least. $\frac{2}{5} \frac{2}{9} \frac{2}{12}$ $\frac{2}{15} \frac{2}{42}$

Circle the best unit for measuring
1. the distance across Africa
centimeters decimeters meters **(kilometers)**
2. the height of a swing set
centimeters decimeters **(meters)** kilometers

Write each number using numerals.
four-fifths $\frac{4}{5}$
two-thirds $\frac{2}{3}$
seven-eighths $\frac{7}{8}$

Solve.
$7)\overline{54}$ = 7 R5
$6)\overline{23}$ = 3 R5

Day #4

Pounds of Recyclables Collected
Comparing totals, the pounds of paper recycled is (>, <, =) the pounds of recycled glass.

These are klinkers.
These are NOT klinkers.
Which of these are klinkers?

There are 1,460 paintings and 3,977 drawings entered in a children's art festival. There were also 315 collages and 89 clay sculptures entered. About how many total entries were there?
- ○ between 5,000 and 6,000
- ● between 6,000 and 7,000
- ○ between 4,000 and 5,000

The chances of drawing a □ are
- ○ greater with box A
- ● greater with box B
- ○ equal with box A or B

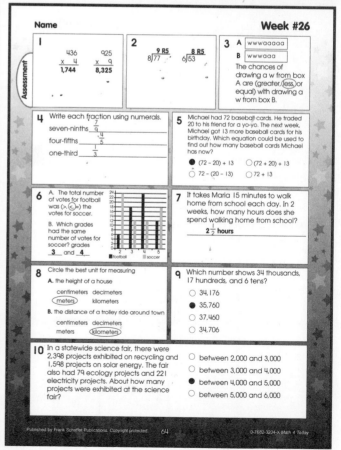

Week #26 (page 64) — Assessment

1. $436 \times 4 = 1,744$ $925 \times 9 = 8,325$

2. $8)\overline{77}$ = 9 R5 $6)\overline{53}$ = 8 R5

3. A wwwaaaa
B wwwaaa
The chances of drawing a w from box A are (greater, **less**, or equal) with drawing a w from box B.

4. Write each fraction using numerals.
seven-ninths $\frac{7}{9}$
four-fifths $\frac{4}{5}$
one-third $\frac{1}{3}$

5. Michael had 72 baseball cards. He traded 20 to his friend for a yo-yo. The next week, Michael got 13 more baseball cards for his birthday. Which equation could be used to find out how many baseball cards Michael has now?
- ● (72 – 20) + 13
- ○ (72 + 20) + 13
- ○ 72 – (20 – 13)
- ○ 72 + 13

6. A. The total number of votes for football was (>, **<**, =) the votes for soccer.
B. Which grades had the same number of votes for soccer? grades **3** and **4**

7. It takes Maria 15 minutes to walk home from school each day. In 2 weeks, how many hours does she spend walking home from school? **2 1/2 hours**

8. Circle the best unit for measuring
A. the height of a house
centimeters decimeters **(meters)** kilometers
B. the distance of a trolley ride around town
centimeters decimeters meters **(kilometers)**

9. Which number shows 34 thousands, 17 hundreds, and 6 tens?
- ○ 34,176
- ● 35,760
- ○ 37,460
- ○ 34,706

10. In a statewide science fair, there were 2,398 projects exhibited on recycling and 1,598 projects on solar energy. The fair also had 79 ecology projects and 221 electricity projects. About how many projects were exhibited at the science fair?
- ○ between 2,000 and 3,000
- ○ between 3,000 and 4,000
- ● between 4,000 and 5,000
- ○ between 5,000 and 6,000

Answer Key

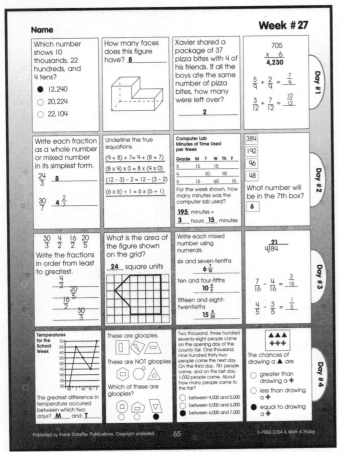

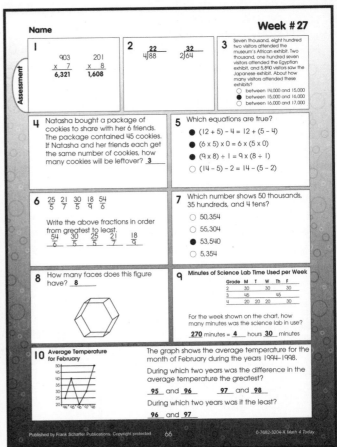

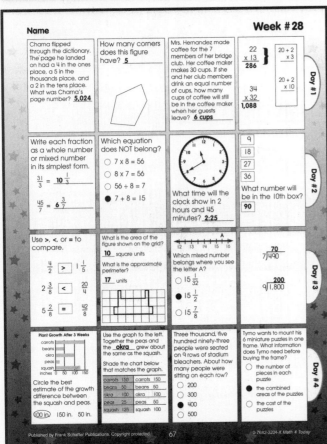

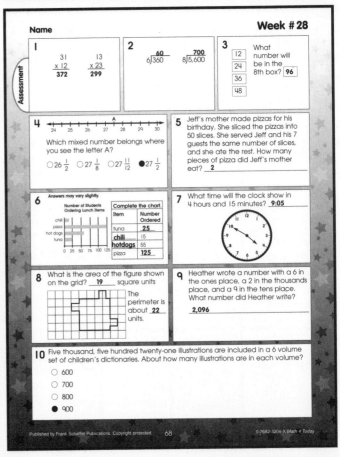

Answer Key

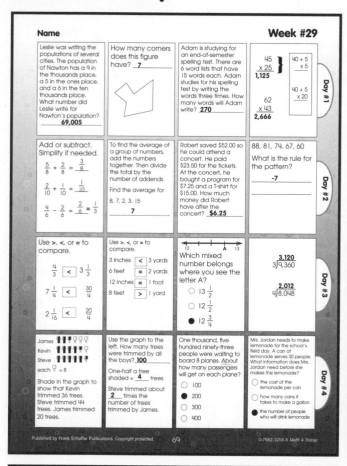

Name   **Week #29**

Leslie was writing the populations of several cities. The population of Nawton has a 9 in the thousands place, a 5 in the ones place, and a 6 in the ten thousands place. What number did Leslie write for Nawton's population? **69,005**

How many corners does this figure have? **7**

Adam is studying for an end-of-semester spelling test. There are 6 word lists that have 15 words each. Adam studies for his spelling test by writing the words three times. How many words will Adam write? **270**

```
  45        40 + 5
 x 25       x 5
1,125
            40 + 5
  62        x 20
 x 43
2,666
```

Day #1

Add or subtract. Simplify if needed.

$\frac{5}{8} + \frac{2}{8} = \frac{7}{8}$

$\frac{2}{10} + \frac{1}{10} = \frac{3}{10}$

$\frac{4}{6} - \frac{2}{6} = \frac{2}{6} = \frac{1}{3}$

To find the average of a group of numbers, add the numbers together. Then divide the total by the number of addends.

Find the average for 8, 7, 2, 3, 15

7

Robert saved $52.00 so he could attend a concert. He paid $23.50 for the tickets. At the concert, he bought a program for $7.25 and a T-shirt for $15.00. How much money did Robert have after the concert? **$6.25**

88, 81, 74, 67, 60

What is the rule for the pattern?

-7

Day #2

Use >, <, or = to compare.

$\frac{9}{3}$ < $3\frac{1}{3}$

$7\frac{1}{4}$ = $\frac{30}{4}$

$2\frac{1}{16}$ < $\frac{20}{4}$

Use >, <, or = to compare.

3 inches < 3 yards
6 feet = 2 yards
12 inches = 1 foot
8 feet > 1 yard

Which mixed number belongs where you see the letter A?

○ $13\frac{1}{2}$
○ $12\frac{1}{2}$
● $12\frac{3}{4}$

```
      3,120
    3)9,360

      2,012
    4)8,048
```

Day #3

James (8 symbols)
Kevin (symbols)
Steve (symbols)

each ♀ = 8

Shade in the graph to show that Kevin trimmed 36 trees. Steve trimmed 44 trees. James trimmed 20 trees.

Use the graph to the left. How many trees were trimmed by all the boys? **100**

One-half a tree shaded = **4** trees

Steve trimmed about **2** times the number of trees trimmed by James.

One thousand, five hundred ninety-three people were waiting to board 8 planes. About how many passengers will get on each plane?

○ 100
● 200
○ 300
○ 400

Mrs. Jordan needs to make lemonade for the school's field day. A can of lemonade serves 30 people. What information does Mrs. Jordan need before she makes the lemonade?

○ the cost of the lemonade per can
○ how many cans it takes to make a gallon
● the number of people who will drink lemonade

Day #4

Published by Frank Schaffer Publications. Copyright protected.   69   0-7682-3204-X *Math 4 Today*

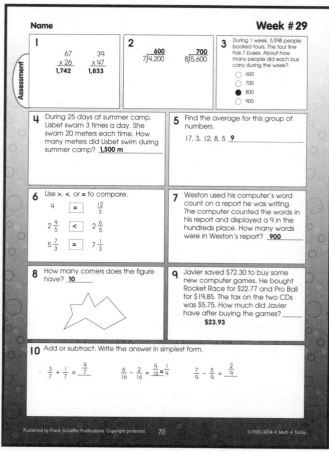

Name   **Week #29**

Assessment

1
```
  67      39
 x 26    x 47
1,742   1,833
```

2
```
    600        700
 7)4,200    8)5,600
```

3 During 1 week, 5,598 people booked tours. The tour line has 7 buses. About how many people did each bus carry during the week?
○ 600
○ 700
● 800
○ 900

4 During 25 days at summer camp, Lisbet swam 3 times a day. She swam 20 meters each time. How many meters did Lisbet swim during summer camp? **1,500 m**

5 Find the average for this group of numbers.
17, 3, 12, 8, 5 **9**

6 Use >, <, or = to compare.
4 = $\frac{12}{3}$
$2\frac{4}{5}$ < $2\frac{6}{5}$
$5\frac{7}{3}$ = $7\frac{1}{3}$

7 Weston used his computer's word count on a report he was writing. The computer counted the words in his report and displayed a 9 in the hundreds place. How many words were in Weston's report? **900**

8 How many corners does the figure have? **10**

9 Javier saved $72.30 to buy some new computer games. He bought Rocket Race for $22.77 and Pro Ball for $19.85. The tax on the two CDs was $5.75. How much did Javier have after buying the games? **$23.93**

10 Add or subtract. Write the answer in simplest form.

$\frac{3}{7} + \frac{1}{7} = \frac{4}{7}$ $\frac{6}{16} - \frac{2}{16} = \frac{4}{16} = \frac{1}{4}$ $\frac{7}{9} - \frac{5}{9} = \frac{2}{9}$

Published by Frank Schaffer Publications. Copyright protected.   70   0-7682-3204-X *Math 4 Today*

Name   **Week #30**

30,000 + 7,000 + 200 + 3 =
○ 37,230
○ 372,003
○ 30,702,003
● 37,203

Write C if the figures are congruent. Write S if they are similar.
C
C
S

Neva bought 3 packages of gum. Each package has 12 pieces. How can Neva share the gum with 8 of her friends so that she and her friends each get the same number of pieces?

36 ÷ 9 = 4

```
  15
 x 75
1,125

 6,247
+4,788
11,035
```

Day #1

Add or subtract. Simplify.

$\frac{5}{12} + \frac{4}{12} = \frac{3}{4}$

$\frac{8}{13} - \frac{5}{13} = \frac{3}{13}$

$\frac{12}{32} + \frac{12}{32} = \frac{3}{4}$

The range of a group of numbers is the difference between the least and the greatest number in the group. The median of a group of numbers is the middle number when the group is arranged from least to greatest.

8, 5, 3, 20, 2

range = **18**
median = **5**

Janette bought nail polish for $3.89, 2 tubes of lip gloss for $2.49 each, and perfume for $9.22. The total after tax was added was $19.54. How much tax did Janette pay on the items she bought?

$1.45

2, 9, 23, 51, 107

What is the rule for the pattern?

+7, +14, +28, + 56...

Day #2

Some of the Largest Earth-Filled Dams Measured in Cubic Yards

Tarbela	186,000,000
Oahe	92,000,000
Cornelia	274,026,000
Pati	261,590
Atatürk	110,522

List the names of the dams in order of size from least to greatest. **Atatürk**

Pati   **Oahe**
Tarbela   **Cornelia**

Use >, <, or = to compare.
24 inches < 3 feet
9 feet > 3 yards
36 inches = 1 yard
10 feet > 2 yards

Which number is read two hundred seventy-five million, nine hundred thousand, forty-six?
● 275,900,046
○ 275,946
○ 200,759,460

```
     905
  5)4,525

     805
  9)7,245
```

Day #3

Margie's Gift Wrapping

Sept.	■ ■ ■ ■ ■
Oct.	■ ■ ■
Nov.	■ ■ ■ ■ ■ ■ ■
Dec.	■ ■ ■ ■ ■ ■ ■ ■

each ■ = 50 gifts wrapped

How many gifts were wrapped in October? **150**

How many gifts were wrapped in September? **225**

Use the graph to the left. How many gifts were wrapped during all four months? **1,125**

How many more gifts were wrapped in November and December than in September? **525**

How many more ■ would be needed to show 250 gifts wrapped in September?

What is 675,789 rounded to the nearest thousand?
○ 700,000
● 676,000
○ 680,000
○ 674,000

Shane spent $25.00 on vacation souvenirs. His mother spent $40.00, and his dad spent $30.00. Judy, Shane's sister, spent more than Shane and Dad but less than Mother. Which could be true?
○ Judy spent $45.00.
● Judy spent $32.00.
○ Judy spent $52.00.

Day #4

Published by Frank Schaffer Publications. Copyright protected.   71   0-7682-3204-X *Math 4 Today*

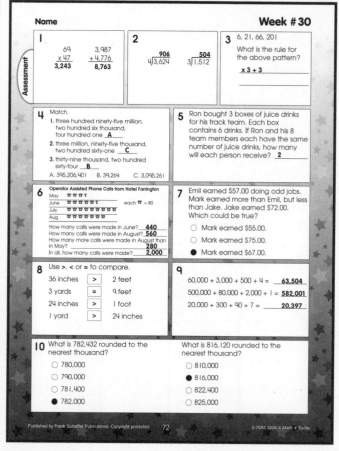

Name   **Week #30**

Assessment

1
```
   69      3,987
  x 47    +4,776
 3,243    8,763
```

2
```
    906        504
 4)3,624    3)1,512
```

3 6, 21, 66, 201
What is the rule for the above pattern?
x 3 + 3

4 Match.
1. three hundred ninety-five million, two hundred six thousand, four hundred one **A**
2. three million, ninety-five thousand, two hundred sixty-one **C**
3. thirty-nine thousand, two hundred sixty-four **B**
A. 395,206,401   B. 39,264   C. 3,095,261

5 Ron bought 3 boxes of juice drinks for his track team. Each box contains 6 drinks. If Ron and his 8 team members each have the same number of juice drinks, how many will each person receive? **2**

6 Operator Assisted Phone Calls from Hotel Farrington

May	☎ ☎ ☎ ☎
June	☎ ☎ ☎ ☎ ☎ ½
July	☎ ☎ ☎ ☎ ☎ ☎ ½
Aug.	☎ ☎ ☎ ☎ ☎ ☎ ☎

each ☎ = 80

How many calls were made in June? **440**
How many calls were made in August? **560**
How many more calls were made in August than in May? **280**
In all, how many calls were made? **2,000**

7 Emil earned $57.00 doing odd jobs. Mark earned more than Emil, but less than Jake. Jake earned $72.00. Which could be true?
○ Mark earned $55.00.
○ Mark earned $75.00.
● Mark earned $67.00.

8 Use >, < or = to compare.
36 inches > 2 feet
3 yards = 9 feet
24 inches > 1 foot
1 yard > 24 inches

9
60,000 + 3,000 + 500 + 4 = **63,504**
500,000 + 80,000 + 2,000 + 1 = **582,001**
20,000 + 300 + 90 + 7 = **20,397**

10 What is 782,432 rounded to the nearest thousand?
○ 780,000
○ 790,000
○ 781,400
● 782,000

What is 816,120 rounded to the nearest thousand?
○ 810,000
● 816,000
○ 822,400
○ 825,000

Published by Frank Schaffer Publications. Copyright protected.   72   0-7682-3204-X *Math 4 Today*

Answer Key

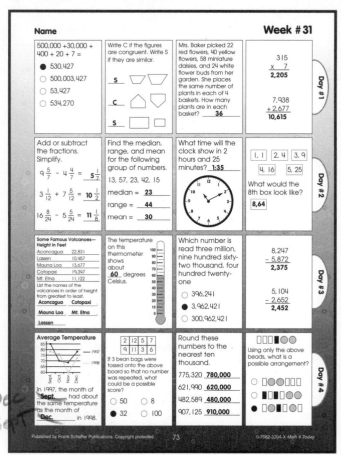

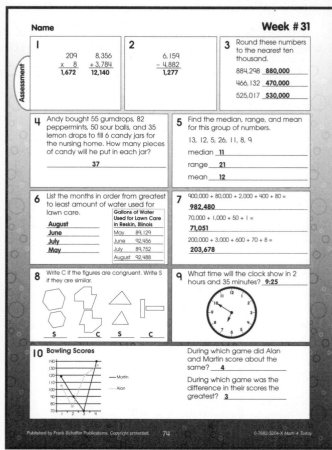

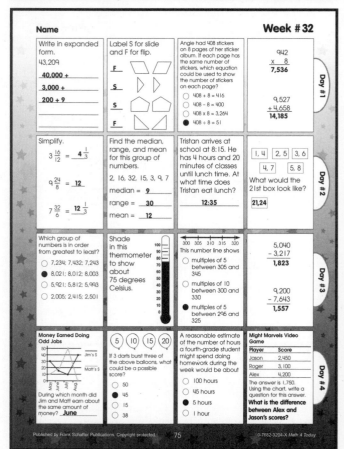

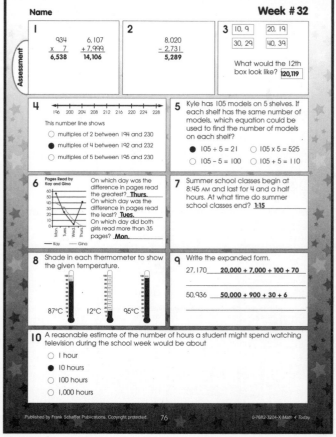

Answer Key

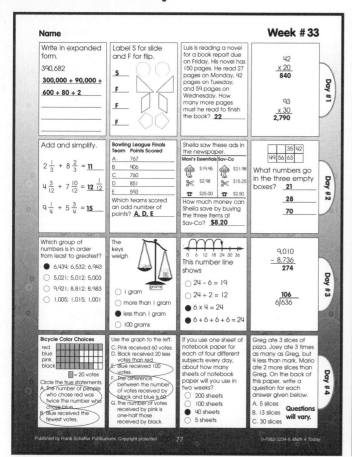

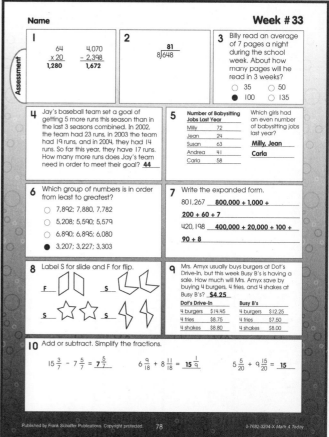

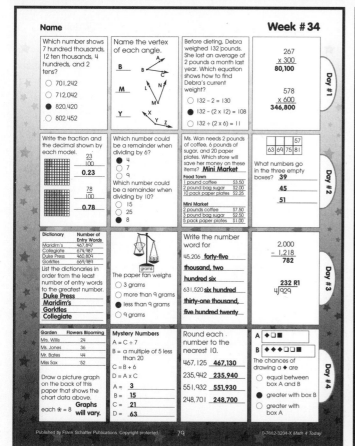

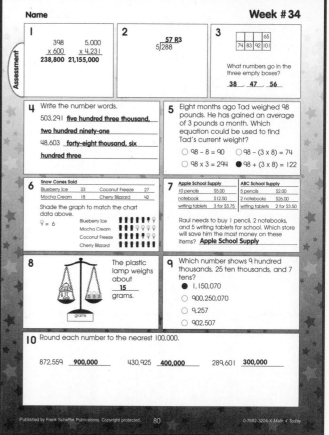

Answer Key

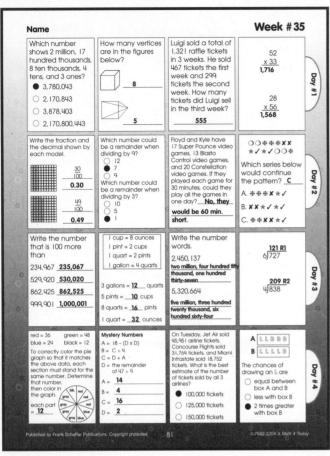

Week #35 (Page 81)

Name — **Week #35**

Day #1

Which number shows 2 million, 17 hundred thousands, 8 ten thousands, 4 tens, and 3 ones?
- ● 3,780,043
- ○ 2,170,843
- ○ 3,878,403
- ○ 2,170,800,443

How many vertices are in the figures below? **8** **5**

Luigi sold a total of 1,321 raffle tickets in 3 weeks. He sold 467 tickets the first week and 299 tickets the second week. How many tickets did Luigi sell in the third week? **555**

52
x 33
1,716

28
x 56
1,568

Day #2

Write the fraction and the decimal shown by each model.
30/100 **0.30**
49/100 **0.49**

Which number could be a remainder when dividing by 9?
- ○ 12
- ● 7
- ○ 9
Which number could be a remainder when dividing by 3?
- ○ 10
- ○ 5
- ● 1

Floyd and Kyle have 17 Super Pounce video games, 13 Blasto Control video games, and 20 Constellation video games. If they played each game for 30 minutes, could they play all the games in one day? **No, they would be 60 min. short.**

○○✶✶✶✕✕
★✓★✓○○✶
Which series below would continue the pattern? **C**
A. ✶✶✶✕★✓
B. ✕✕★✓★✓
C. ✶✶✕✕★✓

Day #3

Write the number that is 100 more than
234,967 **235,067**
529,920 **530,020**
862,425 **862,525**
999,901 **1,000,001**

1 cup = 8 ounces
1 pint = 2 cups
1 quart = 2 pints
1 gallon = 4 quarts
3 gallons = **12** quarts
5 pints = **10** cups
8 quarts = **16** pints
1 quart = **32** ounces

Write the number words.
2,450,137 **two million, four hundred fifty thousand, one hundred thirty-seven**
5,320,664 **five million, three hundred twenty thousand, six hundred sixty-four**

121 R1
6)727

209 R2
4)838

Day #4

red = 36   green = 48
blue = 24   black = 12
To correctly color the pie graph so that it matches the above data, each section must stand for the same number. Determine that number, then color in the graph.
each part = **12**

Mystery Numbers
A = 18 − (D x D)
B = C ÷ 4
C = D + A
D = the remainder of 47 ÷ 9
A = **14**
B = **4**
C = **16**
D = **2**

On Tuesday, Jet Air sold 45,951 airline tickets. Concourse Flights sold 31,764 tickets, and Miami Intrastate sold 18,752 tickets. What is the best estimate of the number of tickets sold by all 3 airlines?
- ● 100,000 tickets
- ○ 125,000 tickets
- ○ 150,000 tickets

A LLBBB
B LLLLB
The chances of drawing an L are
- ○ equal between box A and B
- ○ less with box B
- ● 2 times greater with box B

Week #35 (Page 82)

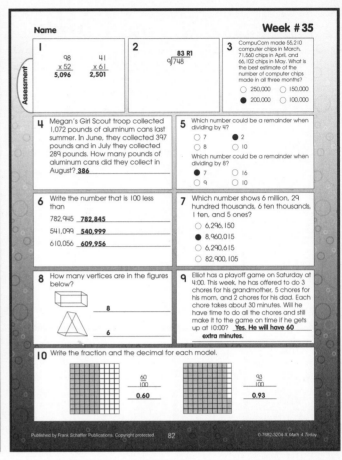

Name — **Week #35**

Assessment

1 98 x 52 = **5,096**   41 x 61 = **2,501**

2 **83 R1** 9)748

3 CompuCom made 55,210 computer chips in March, 71,560 chips in April, and 66,102 chips in May. What is the best estimate of the number of computer chips made in all three months?
- ○ 250,000
- ● 200,000
- ○ 150,000
- ○ 100,000

4 Megan's Girl Scout troop collected 1,072 pounds of aluminum cans last summer. In June, they collected 397 pounds and in July they collected 289 pounds. How many pounds of aluminum cans did they collect in August? **386**

5 Which number could be a remainder when dividing by 4?
- ○ 7
- ● 2
- ○ 8
- ○ 10
Which number could be a remainder when dividing by 8?
- ● 7
- ○ 16
- ○ 9
- ○ 10

6 Write the number that is 100 less than
782,945 **782,845**
541,099 **540,999**
610,056 **609,956**

7 Which number shows 6 million, 29 hundred thousands, 6 ten thousands, 1 ten, and 5 ones?
- ○ 6,296,150
- ● 8,960,015
- ○ 6,290,615
- ○ 82,900,105

8 How many vertices are in the figures below? **8** **6**

9 Elliot has a playoff game on Saturday at 4:00. This week, he has offered to do 3 chores for his grandmother, 5 chores for his mom, and 2 chores for his dad. Each chore takes about 30 minutes. Will he have time to do all the chores and still make it to the game on time if he gets up at 10:00? **Yes. He will have 60 extra minutes.**

10 Write the fraction and the decimal for each model.
60/100 **0.60**
93/100 **0.93**

Week #36 (Page 83)

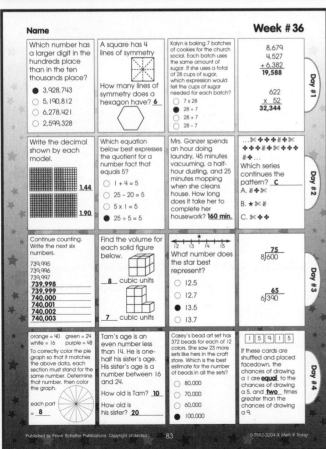

Name — **Week #36**

Day #1

Which number has a larger digit in the hundreds place than in the ten thousands place?
- ● 3,928,743
- ○ 5,190,812
- ○ 6,278,421
- ○ 2,599,328

A square has 4 lines of symmetry.
How many lines of symmetry does a hexagon have? **6**

Kalyn is baking 7 batches of cookies for the church social. Each batch uses the same amount of sugar. If she uses a total of 28 cups of sugar, which expression would tell the cups of sugar needed for each batch?
- ○ 7 x 28
- ● 28 ÷ 7
- ○ 28 + 7
- ○ 28 − 7

8,679
4,527
+ 6,382
19,588

622
x 52
32,344

Day #2

Write the decimal shown by each model.
1.44
1.90

Which equation below best expresses the quotient for a number fact that equals 5?
- ○ 1 + 4 = 5
- ○ 25 − 4 = 5
- ○ 5 x 1 = 5
- ● 25 ÷ 5 = 5

Mrs. Ganzer spends an hour doing laundry, 45 minutes vacuuming, a half-hour dusting, and 25 minutes mopping when she cleans house. How long does it take her to complete her housework? **160 min.**

…★✕✶✶✶✶✶
✶✶✶✶✶✕✶✶✶
✶✶…
Which series continues the pattern? **C**
A. ✶✕✕
B. ★✕✶
C. ✕✶✶

Day #3

Continue counting. Write the next six numbers.
739,995
739,996
739,997
739,998
739,999
740,000
740,001
740,002
740,003

Find the volume for each solid figure below.
8 cubic units
7 cubic units

12 13 14 15
What number does the star best represent?
- ○ 12.5
- ○ 12.7
- ● 13.5
- ○ 13.7

75
8)600

65
6)390

Day #4

orange = 40   green = 24
white = 16   purple = 48
To correctly color the pie graph so that it matches the above data, each section must stand for the same number. Determine that number, then color the graph.
each part = **8**

Tam's age is an even number less than 14. He is one-half his sister's age. She saw 23 more than his sister's age is a number between 16 and 24.
How old is Tam? **10**
How old is his sister? **20**

Casey's bead art set has 372 beads for each of 12 colors. She saw 23 more sets like hers in the craft store. What is the best estimate for the number of beads in all the sets?
- ○ 80,000
- ○ 70,000
- ○ 60,000
- ● 100,000

1 5 9 1 5
If these cards are shuffled and placed facedown, the chances of drawing a 1 are **equal** to the chances of drawing a 5, and **two** times greater than the chances of drawing a 9.

Week #36 (Page 84)

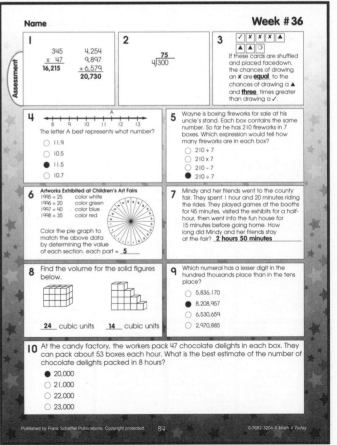

Name — **Week #36**

Assessment

1 345 x 47 = **16,215**   4,254 9,897 + 6,579 = **20,730**

2 **75** 4)300

3 ✓ ✕ ✕ ✕ □
If these cards are shuffled and placed facedown, the chances of drawing an ✕ are **equal** to the chances of drawing a ▲ and **three** times greater than drawing a ✓.

4 8 9 10 11 12 13
The letter A best represents what number?
- ○ 11.9
- ○ 10.5
- ● 11.5
- ○ 10.7

5 Wayne is boxing fireworks for sale at his uncle's stand. Each box contains the same number. So far he has 210 fireworks in 7 boxes. Which expression would tell how many fireworks are in each box?
- ○ 210 + 7
- ○ 210 x 7
- ● 210 ÷ 7
- ○ 210 − 7

6 Artworks Exhibited at Children's Art Fairs
1995 = 25   color white
1996 = 20   color green
1997 = 40   color blue
1998 = 35   color red
Color the pie graph to match the above data by determining the value of each section. each part = **5**

7 Mindy and her friends went to the county fair. They spent 1 hour and 20 minutes riding the rides. They played games at the booths for 45 minutes, visited the exhibits for a half-hour, then went into the fun house for 15 minutes before going home. How long did Mindy and her friends stay at the fair? **2 hours 50 minutes**

8 Find the volume for the solid figures below.
24 cubic units
14 cubic units

9 Which numeral has a lesser digit in the hundred thousands place than in the tens place?
- ○ 5,836,170
- ● 8,208,957
- ○ 6,530,659
- ○ 2,970,885

10 At the candy factory, the workers pack 47 chocolate delights in each box. They can pack about 53 boxes each hour. What is the best estimate of the number of chocolate delights packed in 8 hours?
- ● 20,000
- ○ 21,000
- ○ 22,000
- ○ 23,000

Answer Key

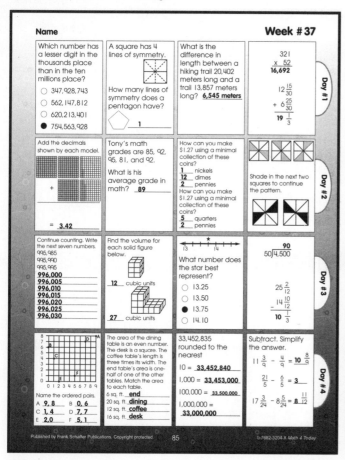

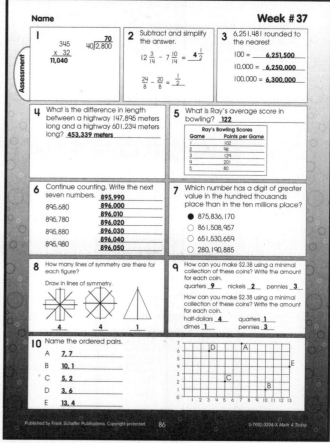

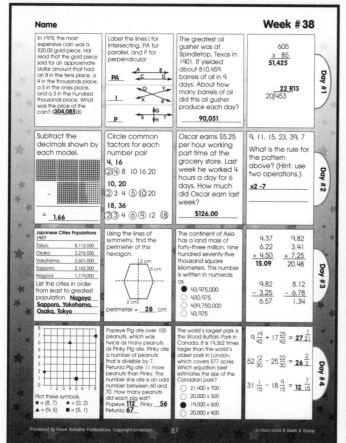

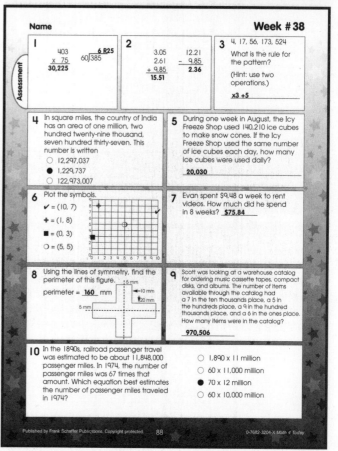

0-7682-3204-X *Math 4 Today*

Answer Key

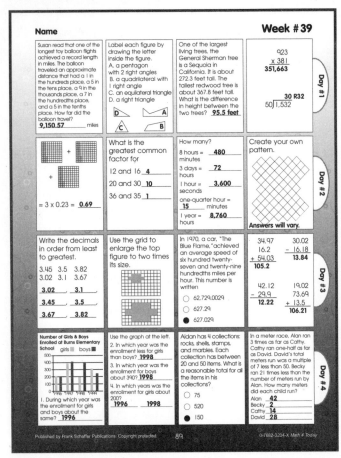

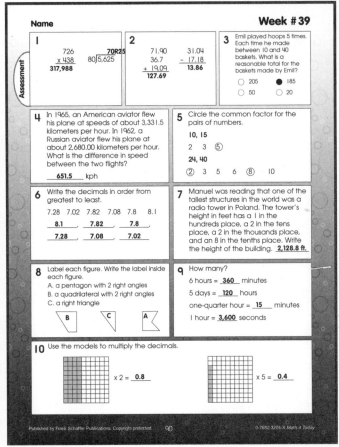

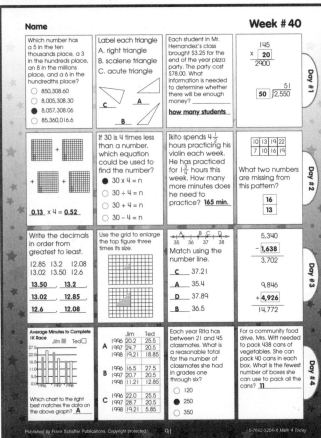

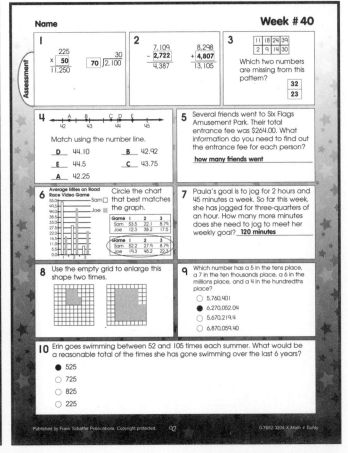

112

0-7682-3204-X *Math 4 Today*